No-Problem
PARENTING

Raising Your Kiddos with More Confidence and Less Fear

PRODUCED BY Jaci Finneman

Edited by Lil Barcaski and Linda Hinkle

Published by: GWN Publishing
www.GWNPublishing.com

Cover Design: Kristina Conatser Captured by KC Designs

ISBN: 979-8-9867817-2-3

This book is dedicated to my mother Cecilia who taught me how to play well with others in the sandbox. To Dawn Cermak who suggested I write the book and introduced me to my publisher Lil Barcaski.

To Lil, your talent speaks for itself, and your heart knows only acceptance, generosity, and belief in the power of stories.

CONTENTS

INTRODUCTION

WORRY IS DRIVEN by fear and fear is fueled by insecurity and uncertainty. Insecure parents' control, hover over, give in, and feel sorry for their children. Lack of confidence can cause shame, embarrassment, resentment, resistance, and even defeat for both the parent and the child.

When we decide to become a parent, we are excited, and although nervous, we often feel well-prepared, anxiously waiting out the last couple of weeks for the baby or child to arrive.

When we unexpectantly become a parent or accept the responsibility of caring for a child that needed a parent, the excitement may sometimes be overshadowed by worry and doubt.

Whatever your level of preparation and excitement or lack thereof, whether we birth our children, step in as another parent to a child in a combined family, foster or adopt – parenting comes with all the feels and few guarantees. And it's difficult.

You don't need to have the experience to be good at it to get the title, "parent," and despite your imperfections, within days or a few weeks, you become an expert of your child.

When I tell my parent-coaching clients that "you are the expert on your child" many respond, "then why isn't my parenting working"?

The answer to that is often one of three things:

1. You're being too nice
2. You're being too mean
3. You're trying to solve a problem that you're not skilled at and attempting to go it alone.

> The definition of expert that I'm referring to is having, involving, or displaying special skill or *knowledge* derived from training or *experience*

Just because we are the "experts" on our children doesn't mean we know them inside and out their entire childhood, doesn't mean we *have* to know everything about them, and certainly doesn't mean we have to become the expert in helping them.

Being the expert on your child often means you have a connection and intuition, a gut feeling; you know when something isn't right, you can feel their sadness and their happiness. You know their cues, their coos, and what they are meaning to say via their facial expressions and their posture.

Do you believe you are the expert on your child? Do you feel confident in your ability to care for and advocate for your child? Are you unsure if you are making the best decisions, using the best techniques, and having the right conversations? Are you doubting your decisions, relying on family, friends, and professionals for their expert advice even when you know their advice won't work? Do you just hope someone will step in and "fix" or solve your child or family's problems?

Let's boost your confidence and get you feeling capable of leading your kids, helping them to learn how to grow into responsible respectful people who are confident in their abilities. Let's kick all things fear and insecurity to the curb.

I designed this book to show you how it is possible to be the expert of your child while accessing outside support from niched experts who understand and acknowledge the vital role of parents in their child's lives. In other words, the authors in this book are not here to solve the problem for you, but rather, with you. You get to be the expert on your child and they are the expert in their craft or calling. These experts have their own stories and, personal and professional experiences which called them or led them to serve others who can relate.

The authors in this book exude the *No-Problem Parenting*™ approach and I am confident in their ability to support you.

If you are new to the *No-Problem Parenting*™ three-step approach:

1. **SEEK FIRST TO UNDERSTAND**, "why is my child behaving the way they are and why am I as the parent responding (or reacting) the way I am."

2. **PREPARE FOR THE WORST.** As parents, we can't always be prepared for the curve balls that life and our children throw our way, and there are lots of behaviors that happen consistently so we can be prepared to respond vs react.

3. **CHANGE THE CONVERSATION:** No-Problem parents lead with empathy, understanding, and guidance. We do not believe in fear-based tactics, rather, in matter of fact, cause and effect, conditional and unconditional communication.

Each author has written their chapter around these three steps and I am grateful to each one of them for sharing their resources with my *No-Problem Parenting*™ Community via this book, being a guest on The *No-Problem Parenting™* Podcast, and as a member of our resource community at noproblemparents.com

I hope this book inspires you and provides education and a new perspective that will have you feeling confident in areas of parenting that you otherwise felt insecure about. And I hope you will reach out to the authors for you and/or your child. Invite the authors into your community of parents, schools, workplaces, and churches. They are from around the world and are willing to travel and/or provide virtual training and presentations.

For updates on all that *No-Problem Parenting™* has to offer, go to **www.noproblemparents.com**

JACI FINNEMAN

This chapter is dedicated to the misunderstood and judged moms and dads caring for children who have endured early life trauma. I see you, I hear you and I Thank You for loving them even when they don't love you back.

NO-PROBLEM PARENTING™ BUILDS TRUST BETWEEN PARENTS AND THEIR DEFIANT OR WITHDRAWN CHILD

by *Jaci Finneman*

"Begin with the end in mind."

—STEPHEN R. COVEY

IN MY WORK with children who have experienced a disrupted attachment in their first few years of life with their birth mom, I often lead with empathy for the parents and the child. I approach this in the same way, whether you are a birth parent, foster or adoptive parent, stepparent or you work with children where during your work hours you are a child's primary caregiver (i.e., daycare provider, nanny, teacher, group home or residential home provider etc.).

Learning about and understanding the *First Year of Life Bonding Cycle* is key to building trust between children and their caregivers.

The *First Year of Life* bonding cycle starts with a baby's needs and tuning in to how the baby expresses their needs in a variety of non-verbal ways. When parents understand the baby's cues and how the full bonding cycle works, parenting becomes less emotionally challenging.

"WHAT DO BABIES DO TO LET THEIR CAREGIVER KNOW THEY HAVE A NEED?" They *cry*. They cannot talk so they cry. What if mom is in the shower or dad has something cooking on the stove and can't get to the baby right away? They cry harder. And, if the baby's need is great enough, the baby cries so hard, they "rage." The baby's face turns deep red, their body stiffens, they arch their back, and sometimes the little baby must catch their breath from crying so hard.

WHAT DOES THE CAREGIVER DO TO MEET THE BABY'S NEEDS? We pick them up, feed them, rock them, change their diaper, and comfort them. This is called *Gratification*! The caregiver picks the baby up, smiles at them, says "shhh, shhh, shhh," while gently bouncing them in their arms with movement. We change the baby's diaper, gently touch the baby, sometimes kissing their little face or stroking their cheek with a soft touch of our hand. We hold the baby up close in our arms, looking at the baby as if to say, "you're ok, you're gonna be ok," with loving *eye contact*.

When this happens, the baby soothes, calms, and even smiles back as if to say "I trust you." The baby learns that when they have a need, they will be cared for. They learn that when they are hungry mom will feed them, their tummy will feel warm and settled, and then looking into the parent's eyes, they internalize you as the person responsible for the good feeling they are having. The baby begins to trust.

This gratification cycle happens thousands of times over the baby's first year of life. The mom learns every day, every moment, the baby's sounds, and movements, what their coos mean or what their body movements mean. Is my baby hungry? Is my baby scared? Is my baby in pain? The caretaker figures it out, meets the need, and this reciprocal non-verbal language is what builds trust. Baby associates the caregiver with the good feeling they are having and learns that it is safe to trust adults. And trust is what connects us, bonds us, and ATTACHES us.

But what happens when the attachment/trust is disrupted? What if there is a break in the cycle between the baby's cries and gratification? When a baby is born premature, as tiny as a pound, doctors can save that baby. But the baby's skin isn't developed, so if it's touched it would burn. The baby is nursed to health, which is a miracle but for some babies, the trauma of the pain causes them to lack trust in adults.

When a parent cannot seem to soothe a baby due to colic or other medical pain, the baby may internalize the parent as the source of the pain and reject the parents attempts at comforting them. When a mother is suffering from post-partum depression and is struggling to connect with her baby emotionally, even though she is still feeding and changing the baby, the connection through the eyes and comforting touch is not there. Often, when the mother recovers, she blames herself, is ashamed or incredibly sad for her child, and does everything to comfort and appease the baby through toddlerhood, unknowingly teaching the child they are the leader.

Disruptions or breaks in attachment and connection, include early separation from their birth mom, death of the birth mom, adoption (when the mother couldn't care for the baby and her only option *or her best decision* was to give her child up for adoption), premature birth, medical pain, multiple caregivers/

daycare providers or when the baby was abused, neglected or removed from the home.

When any of these experiences happen, regardless of good intention by the caregivers, professionals or authorities, it can cause a break in attachment. I share this not to make the reader "feel bad", rather, because knowledge is key, and the more we know, the better we understand, and the more we can help the children and parents affected by the affects of early life breaks in attachment.

When between the *crying* and the *gratification* there is a break. If the mom consistently doesn't come when the baby is crying, when the loving parent does try but cannot soothe the baby's pain, when the parent doesn't feed the baby when s/he is hungry because it's not time yet, or the baby sits in their wet diaper for long hours or in the car seat or swing without human connection. If gratification doesn't happen or is not consistent; when the caregiver finally does meet the need, the baby does not internalize the caregiver as the source of good feelings. The baby does not learn to trust that the parent is good. Instead, the baby learns that s/he is responsible for getting her/his needs met. Even though the caretaker does eventually feed them or change their diaper, the baby will often not look into the caretaker's eyes for fear of further rejection or pain. The baby begins to grieve and sometimes becomes fearful. The fear is because while the baby desperately wants the comfort and love of their caretaker, they cannot risk being rejected again and thus have learned to self-soothe.

If/when the baby is removed from the birth mother's care, the new mother/caretaker must learn the baby's cues all over again. The baby, having been abandoned by their unable or unwilling birth mother, rejects the new mother because the primal brain remembers the rejection or inconsistency and is fearful to let that happen to them again. So, the baby continues to self-soothe.

The mother is confused by the baby's unwillingness to be held and comforted. She attempts to let the baby take the lead and describes the baby as being very independent. The baby holds its own bottle, does not give eye contact, does not want to be held, and seems settled when left to his own devices. As the baby grows to toddlerhood, they rarely accept the word "no," especially from the mother or primary figure. The baby learns to get their own needs/wants met by becoming demanding and is able to charm others into getting what s/he needs/wants.

As the toddler grows, they become resentful and even envious of the other children in the home; birth siblings, foster siblings, and even children in daycare or school. They become envious of the children that feel love and have a relationship with their mother. They resent the mother even more. If the child was adopted, they resent the birth mother too, however, the love for her is still strong, as they are still grieving her. The child may become hurtful to other children who know how to love and accept love. The hurt child wants the other children to (consciously or unconsciously) hurt as they do. They see the parents loving on the other children and they become angry. They want the mother/parent to hurt as they hurt. So, the disrupted attachment cycle continues.

Whether you are the birth parent, adoptive or foster parent, or relative caregiver, the earlier you understand your child's first year of life experience, the better equipped you will be to support and nurture them. Do not try to rescue a child who suffered a break in attachment from the reality of their experience. Even though it may be uncomfortable and painful for you as you feel heartbreak for your child's trauma and grief, it is their reality, their story. It will, however, require more than unconditional love. They need your understanding and confident leadership. They need to know you can handle their painful and often dark thoughts. They need to know you are safe and will do whatever it takes to keep them safe, even from themselves.

Here are three things parents should avoid with a child who rejects their love and traditional parenting (has had a break in attachment with their primary caregiver) and what you can do instead:

1. **CONVINCING, NEGOTIATING, OR PERSUADING** the child to do something or stop doing something. Offering logical, reasonable, or practical advice and information works with many littles and even teenagers, but not for most kids with breaks in attachment.

   > **INSTEAD**: Be clear about your expectations without injecting strong emotions (i.e., sadness or anger). Approach your instructions with a "matter of fact," straightforward expectation and direction. Be clear and concise.

2. **REACTING WITH ANGER/DISAPPOINTMENT/SADNESS**: Inserting your emotions, especially reactively, with a fight/flight/freeze response (FFF), activates your child's FFF and triggers the child to defend themselves. The natural result is for the parent to respond with defense, and you'll find yourself in a tug of war to win control. Your child will likely experience your frustration and anger as proof that they (the kiddo) are effectively controlling you, and the parents' emotions, and will see you as insecure, incapable, and unsafe.

   > **INSTEAD**: Pause before responding when you are upset or sad. It takes just six seconds to calm your amygdala, the smoke detector of your brain that alerts you that

you are being challenged. When you take just six seconds to pause and breathe, you calm your central nervous system enough to decide whether the behavior warrants immediate action, or it can wait until you've had time to think about it. If there is a safety concern, of course, you need to respond right away. If not, most responses can wait until you and your child are calm and not reactive.

3. **FEELING SORRY FOR AND RESCUING** your child from the consequences of their behavior and/or attempting to solve your kiddo's problems for them.

INSTEAD: Help your child solve the problem themselves. Be empathetic that owning up to the problem they caused themselves or others is hard. Let them know that once they make right what they did wrong, they will feel better. Rescuing your child from their mistakes or misbehavior only delays the gratification that they are capable of solving their problems and often creates anxiety and lack of confidence or belief in themselves and their ability.

As a 30-year Counselor turned Parent Coach, I have supported hundreds of parents whose children suffer from disrupted attachment and who have been misunderstood and mistreated by the mental health system (child and parent alike). Children who reject traditional parenting because of their understandable lack of trust in adults, have caused many nurturing parents to become enraged and strict, often resentful of the child. These real-life examples are often too painful for non-traumatized people to accept, including professionals. Our heart strings are tugged, and we want to help in traditional loving ways that, alone, simply do not actually help these children or their parents and families.

Parents and children deserve to be understood and accommodated with the goal of keeping families together whenever possible. And problems are meant to be dealt with and overcome. Trauma is not a life sentence. When we seek first to understand why our child is behaving or responding the way they are, we can parent with understanding, consistency, and empathetic leadership.

Hello World and *No-Problem Parenting*™ started in 2013 with a mission of "awakening attachment" and focused on coaching parents whose children suffered early breaks in attachment. In 2018, after being encouraged by many parents with children experiencing "typical behavior problems," who said, "well if you can help families who have suffered tremendous pain and trauma, why can't you help us?", we now coach all parents; teaching you and supporting you in becoming the confident leader your kids crave you to be. With over 40,000 hours of experience working directly with families in their homes, we know there is a solution for any behavioral problem you are experiencing.

To become a part of the *No-Problem Parenting*™ Community, visit **www.noproblemparenting.com** and to learn more about 1:1 parent coaching and resources go to **www.noproblemparents.com**

TRICIA PARIDO

I dedicate this chapter to my husband and our children who have supported me with unconditional positive regard in my journey to living authentically, in concrete contentment, free from conditioned behavior, and released from past programming.

TLR: THE LIFE REcovery PROCESS

by *Tricia Parido*

I get the battle! I know the internal hell you wish would just stop! It's hard to stop drinking, dieting, binging, splurging, and giving away all your time and energy.

We're bombarded with so many pressures in our lives, it's hard to keep up.

Parenting is not an easy task at the best of times but when you are juggling work pressure and family stresses alongside your own mental health. It can feel impossible! But there are ways around this!

Did you know **HABITS, NEGATIVE ATTACHMENTS,** and **ADDICTIONS** can be overcome?

I do! Because I did it!

It doesn't matter how long you have been holding on to them or using them to cope with your emotions or life stressors. You **CAN** drop them all **AND** live for yourself first **WITHOUT** feeling guilty, selfish, punished, or restricted.

And what's even better.

You can keep those things you love; you just need to change your relationship with them.

I want to be the first person to tell you this... **There are No "good" habits!** Trust me you want to learn why living without habits fixes **EVERYTHING!**

BUT... Change won't arrive without action.

Hey there! I'm Tricia Parido, a Fierce Optimist who loves to help change lives!

I have walked every corner of Life Recovery personally and professionally; I have combined my journey with trauma, addictions, eating disorders, negative attachments, and countless habits with my 25+ year life recovery journey and in-depth degree studies to create an intimate interactive experience designed to be focused on life going forward, transforming emotional intelligence, and generating a healthy lifestyle for any life recovery journey.

Are you experiencing any of these issues?

- You rely on alcohol to calm frustration and stress
- Living with people-pleasing codependency—your self-worth and value comes from what you do for others
- Battling with your relationship with food and the all-in or all-out dieting culture
- Fighting with impulse control like shopping or anything else that is lacking discipline
- Struggling with behavioral issues—a need to be right OR bothered by things you cannot control
- Lacking life skills—you are constantly on an emotional rollercoaster

- Or are simply feeling stuck

Here are a few of the top outcomes TLR clients are sharing:

"Self-Acceptance"

"Personal Acknowledgement"

"Celebrating My Wins"

"Living in the moment"

"Slowing Down and Staying Present"

"I feel seen, heard, accepted, confident, and valued"

"I know I am valid"

"I have Clarity"

"I am Resilient"

"I make intuitive decisions"

"I am grateful for my Recovery Journey"

My laser coaching WILL get you unstuck so you can effectively manage your life structure and begin living your days being the best you. More specifically we work together to **Transform** how you see yourself experiencing living, how you experience your environment, and how others experience you. You will **Attain** the esteem you need to create the voice you desire that will foster the unveiling of your dreams. And you will learn to be who and how you want to be in all categories of your life with lifelong **Maintainability.**

If you have gotten this far and are still with me, you are probably thinking OK great thanks but **how is any of this going to help me with why my child behaves the way they do and why do I react the way I do?**

I would like to start with a known to be true reason.

Conditioning!

Think back to your childhood, how you communicated with your parents and them with you. Maybe even go back a bit further to how perhaps your parents and their parents communicated. Is there a common theme or thread? Was there a bit of the old "do as I say not as I do" attitude in there anywhere?

Now ask yourself again what is it that my child does that prompts my reactivity? And why am I so reactive to it?

If I had to guess it falls in some version of the "don't talk back, be respectful, do as I say" conditioned way of being that has filtered down (and maybe even softened) over the years and through generations.

But I promise it is definitely more about you than it is your child.

Your reactivity, even when it follows your child's behavior, is what is crippling the relationship and causing the discomfort you are experiencing and thereby the continued issues inside of your home.

Your child is being led by you. They learn their attitudes and behaviors at home first, they add in outside influence later. Notice the word add. They already have what they learned at home and then in their desire for autonomy and individuality make tweaks and adjustments along the way.

This is a very top-level example but all the reason why at TLR all of our clients begin in a space of getting to know themselves at a level they had never considered. This is very necessary so we can see where cultivating the art of pause is needed and gain the ability to be responsive in all things we do (notice I did not say react).

Here are a few scenarios I hear often; I'm worried about my adolescent, they seem to be isolating, they don't have a friend base, they aren't physically active, they are gaining weight, they are always complaining about being bored, they only eat junk food, or they don't eat at all, I've noticed some significant attitude shifts, I think they may be vaping, using marijuana, and I'm pretty sure they are drinking alcohol out of our cabinet.

It's here where I redirect back to you.

What example are you leading by? Are you normalizing any of these things in those examples?

Ask yourself; What do I rely on to bring me peace joy comfort or relief? Is it alcohol? Do you use marijuana?

What about your relationship with food? Do you eat for comfort?

Do you treat a good week or a bad day with a bottle of wine, a visit to the local creamery?

Is your relationship with health and fitness an all-in or an all-out relationship? How is your body image? What does it sound like out loud when you talk about yourself?

Yes! This is where we will together dive in and look at how you operate. What things outside of yourself have been given an emotional purpose that are inappropriate. (a bottle of wine for stress relief is inappropriate. A glass of wine that pairs well with your steak is appropriate).

We also need to examine your language. That's right, how you communicate with yourself and others. What are you sending out? Plus, how do you hear. This is imperative. That way you no longer operate from a stance of a judger, someone who takes things personally, is rigid in their beliefs and expectations.

But instead, you become a person, a parent, who maneuvers through life in an open stance, what I refer to as the stance of a learner, where you seek deeper understanding and an expanded consciousness.

I can't give you everything in this limited space that you need to reduce your vulnerability and reactivity so you can purposefully regulate your emotions. But I can give you some tips that will help you face the distress in parenting, find resolution, and incorporate tactics of assertiveness.

1. **Take a breath.** Just because your child has a need or is in a heightened state does not mean you need to join them there. You need time to get into the proper headspace, or stance as I mentioned above. So create the space you need to give them what they need.

   a. Using a response like; I hear that you are bothered, I want to give you my full attention, I will meet you in your room in 10 minutes. Or, I have a hard time following you when you are this upset, can you take 10 min to breathe and just be still in your room, I will come listen to you after you are calmed down.

2. **Take a beat.** Just because you are in a heightened state, have had a stressful day, are feeling spent, taken for granted, or ... doesn't mean that your child doesn't need you to show up supportive, patient, or of sound mind. So, create the space you need to give what they need.

   a. Using language like; I am excited to hear about your day and to help you with what you need, I do however need a few moments to clear my mind. I had a stressful day, and I don't want my irritation from work to be a part of our conversation.

3. **Create space.** Arguing takes two. Create effective limits and limitations for yourself. Asking for a pause in any con-

versation that is going in the wrong direction is extremely useful. Especially if the person getting ready to raise their voice and dig their heels in is you!

4. **Hear softer.** The filter you are listening through can change everything. Listen in such a way that they cannot help but excel in your presence. Choosing to be dedicated to listen for the others brilliance, for what is already right, good, and perfect. Then celebrate before offering your refinement. The improvement or clarification of something by the making of small changes, the removal of impurities or unwanted elements from a substance.

5. **Speak clearer.** True assertiveness is more than direct communication. It is open honest genuine transparent and authentic communication. You have the opportunity here to expand your consciousness, face distress gracefully and reduce vulnerability. Think of yourself and your audience. How do I want to see myself and how do I want to be received?

"When you dream about what you aspire to
attain you are more apt to create effective action
to make your dreams a maintainable reality"

—TP

As a Life Recovery Master, I speak with women who are wives and mothers, men who are husbands and fathers, as well as professionals.

AND WHAT I SEE IS...

Anxiety and overwhelm are very prevalent especially when you feel immense pressure to perform.

What if I told you that it's all simply your desire to find your place in the world that creates a desire to escape?

The *challenge* is that you don't know how to move from anxiety and overwhelm to joy and freedom. The reason for this is simple, it's the past programming that you are not aware of that is holding you back!

The good news is I can identify your biggest emotional block in 30 minutes or less. All you need to do now is email me at **turningleavesrecovery@gmail.com** with the words "*My Awakening Call*" and I'll send you a complimentary link to get your answer.

CHANGE WON'T ARRIVE WITHOUT ACTION! THERE MUST BE MOVEMENT!

I invite you to EVOLVE. The process has changed every relationship I have. Most importantly the relationship between myself my husband our 5 children and 5 grandchildren. And it has provided the same for thousands of other adults.

Believe me, you need you to be the best version of yourself you can be. And if you can trust me, I want to show you how to comfortably move through the uncomfortable.

I have bridged the gap for you so your journey to relief can be a direct path to your freedom and in a much shorter process than my own. Together we will:

- Create A Solid Foundation
- Maximize Maintainable Momentum
- Leverage Your Personal Strengths
- Strategize Systems To Optimize Your Functioning
- Synthesize Your Life Stories

- Strengths, Skill, Satisfactions
- Discover What You Truly Need, Want, & Desire
- Release The Fears Holding You Back
- Investigate Old Ways Of Being And
- Internalize New Ways Of Becoming

My laser coaching will get you unstuck so you can effectively manage your life structure and begin living your days weeks months being the best you you can be.

It's impactful!

If you are ready to learn the practical application of the effective psychological life skills and tactics, gain esteem building momentum, live with consistency and lead by great example, I'm ready for you.

All you need to do now is email me at **turningleavesrecovery@ gmail.com** with the words *"My Awakening Call"* and I'll send you a complimentary link to get your answer.

Tricia Parido BS Psych, IMAC, NCPLC, CATCIII, NCIP, NCP-CM
Founder | Master Coach
Turning Leaves Recovery Life and Wellness Coaching
(805) 710-2513

FIND ME
turningleavesrecovery@gmail.com
https://www.linkedin.com/in/triciaparido/
https://www.turningleavesrecovery.com/

SANDRA DAVIS

Dedicated to my husband, two children, and all families around the world with love

PARENT AND CHILD RELATIONSHIPS

by *Sandra Davis*

FOR OVER 20 YEARS, I have been facilitating and supporting leadership development and business cultures to thrive and have consulted with companies in New Zealand, Australia, Malaysia, Singapore, The Caribbean, Guyana, Brazil, and the USA.

With a Diploma of Facilitation and a passion for coaching, instructional design, and curriculum development, I am committed to empowering people to lead happy and enriched lives. I have designed tools and resources that support others to become "People-literate" (the understanding of self and others), for creating lives that are rewarding - both personal and professional by applying the *DISC Behavioral Model and Method*.

I am also a trained facilitator for *"The Virtues Project,"* a global initiative founded by Linda Kavelin-Popov, which provides multicultural programs and materials that empower people to remember who they really are and to live by their highest values. I am the Co-Founder and CEO of PeopleSmart Enterprises LLC, the co-creator of the *"PeopleSmart DISC Interpretation Meth-*

od" and the Co-Founder of PeopleSmart Academy which offers online courses for teaching *People-literacy.* I am also the creator of the *"DISCovering Me Program for Youth."*

If people were to ask what my personal vision was, it would be to empower families and youth to lead productive, happy, and successful lives—relationships that are filled with love and understanding.

In 2015-16, I was asked to deliver several workshops over a nine-week period to a small rural school in Auckland, NZ. I had been delivering leadership and management training to staff, and the Deputy Principal asked if I could teach DISC communication and leadership skills to his students aged 11-13 years because he had gained so much benefit from his interactions with me. At the time, there were also issues with bullying in the school.

Here's where it gets interesting.

Having a background in instructional design and training, I successfully designed and delivered a nine-week leadership, communication skills, and character development program using the DISC Behavioral Model and an anti-bullying program (eight 90-minute workshops) to 25 students that became the *"DISCovering Me*™ Program for Youth." Since then, other programs that include online assessments, teacher online training, teacher and student resources, and tools have been developed for older students, 13 years plus.

In 2020, we were thrown into a global pandemic, and the parenting world as we know it changed. Mothers, fathers, caregivers, daughters, sons, and siblings were thrown into isolation with very little warning. I'm sure parents said to themselves, "Help, now what do I do?" In lockdown, unfortunately, I said to myself, "Well, Sandra, you're not lazy, you're just highly motivated to do nothing." Oops! Being a High S-Dove style in lockdown, (We'll get to learn about the DISC Behavioral Model and the four Bird styles soon), all I seemed to be doing was cleaning up after everyone and making sure we didn't run out of food or get Covid.

My hope for writing this chapter is that you do something with the tips and strategies I'm going to teach you. These tips and strategies will support you to understand what is driving your child's behavior — "Oh, and by the way, yours as well," based on the needs, emotions, and fears of their observable behavior and personality style. They will also give you a way to respond in a more confident and empathetic way when those curve balls are thrown your way.

So, let's get started, shall we? I'd like to introduce you to the DISC Behavioral Model and the four Bird Styles: D-Eagle, I-Parrot, S-Dove, and C-Owl.

THE FOUR DISC BIRD STYLES

The DISC Behavioral Model has been around since the 1920's. It was first developed by a man named William Moulton Marsden.

In the DISC Model of Observable Behavior, there are four Primary Styles: Dominance, Influence, Steadiness, and Compliance and each one reacts a certain way when under stress. Before I explain when and how each style reacts, remember I mentioned about the four bird styles? So think about these four birds again. Now we're going to relate them to the four Primary DISC styles. Here they are: **EAGLE** is for Dominance, **PARROT** is for Influence, **DOVE** is for Steadiness and **OWL** is for Compliance.

We start to shape our DISC Bird Style from a very early age. If you have a 2 to 3-year-old, you may have noticed if they are outgoing or not, or if they want their own way all the time or are happy to cooperate. At about the age of 10-12 years, we pretty much have shaped who we are based on our DISC Primary Bird Style. Each of these four styles have needs, emotions, and fears that drive their behavior.

As a parent, if you want to deepen your understanding of how our personality interacts in relationships, you need to understand these four styles. Here's a quick overview of each style's needs, emotions, and fears:

	D-EAGLE	I-PARROT	S-DOVE	C-OWL
DISC Focus	*Problems*	*People*	*Pace*	*Procedures*
NEEDS	Challenges to solve and being in charge	Social relationships and friendly environment	Systems, team and stable environments	Rules to follow and data to analyze
EMOTIONS	Anger and Impatience	Optimism and Trust	Patience and Non-Expression	Fear and Concern
FEARS	Being taken advantage of/lack of control	Being left out/ loss of social approval	Sudden change/loss of stability and security	Being criticized/loss of accuracy and quality

Here's a bird's eye view of the traits, personal strengths, and fears for each Bird Style. I've also added a tip for each of the styles. When you're reading these, you might start to see yourself and your children in a different way. Also, try to remember each Bird's overview, as it will help you to communicate more effectively with each Bird style.

D EAGLES LIKE TO FOCUS ON TASKS AND ARE FAST PACED

They are naturally competitive, results orientated, innovative and direct. Great at solving problems is a strength of this style. They fear loss of control and under stress, may become dictatorial.

> TIP: Eagle Styles would benefit from practicing patience by calmly tolerating a delay or confusion, and by accepting things they cannot control with humor and grace. And those of you who identify with the Eagles, remember that tolerance is respecting the opinions of others when they are different from yours.

I PARROTS LIKE TO FOCUS ON PEOPLE AND ARE ALSO FAST PACED

They are naturally confident, trusting, optimistic and sociable and can motivate others by their enthusiasm, a strength of this style. They fear being rejected and socially disapproved of, and under stress, will become superficial and sarcastic.

> TIP: Parrot Styles would benefit from practicing self-discipline by not being so overly emotional and by not having to seek approval all the time. If you think you are a Parrot, use detachment so that your emotions won't control you. Start creating routines for yourself and keep the agreements you make with others in your family.

S DOVES ALSO LIKE TO FOCUS ON PEOPLE AND ARE SLOW PACED

They are naturally understanding, friendly, patient and team players and are known for being supporters and good listeners, both strengths of this style. They fear sudden change and, under stress, will become submissive and indecisive.

> **TIP**: Dove Styles would benefit from practicing assertiveness when pressured by sharing their own ideas and feelings and by tactfully asking for what they want. If you think you're a Dove and need support, ask for it, because us Doves tend to take on steadying everything in our family and take responsibility for doing it all!

C OWLS LIKE TO FOCUS ON TASKS AND ARE ALSO SLOW PACED

They are naturally detailed, courteous, fact finders and compliant and like to organize and plan when it comes to the details of a task. These are strengths of this style. They fear being wrong and can become too critical and impersonal. They are also their own worst inner critic and need to worry less about everything.

> **TIP**: Owl Styles would benefit from practicing trust by having the confidence that the right thing will come about without worrying and trusting in their own abilities - knowing they are perfect just the way they are. If you think you're an Owl, learn to open up and share your feelings more. Find the joy in life and let that joy be felt by your family. You know those moments where you tell a joke with your kids or pull a funny face at the dinner table, just because you can!

So, can you see why it is that you respond or react the way you do sometimes as a parent. We all have strengths and fears that make us who we are. The DISC Model is situational, so depending on what situation you find yourself in will depend on how you act or react.

EACH BIRD'S CHARACTER VIRTUE STRENGTHS

Your DISC behavioral style is how you DO things – those behavioral habits are how you do things automatically without thinking. And they are observable by others. But if you think about the people you really admire, you'll find that what makes someone popular, successful, and self-confident are the qualities they are BEING – assertive, friendly, patient, responsible or diligent.

I'd like to now introduce you to each Bird style's Character Virtue Strengths. These are certain qualities that are well developed in your personality and that come easily to you. These unique strengths make it easy for you to excel in certain activities more than others such as Problems, People, Pace or Procedures.

There are times when each of the styles secretly **WISH** they could be just like someone else. Do you? It's natural to think like this, and everyone does sometimes. It just takes one more step in the process of **SELF-DISCOVERY**, called identifying and practicing the Character Virtues that will give you and your children the results you seek.

HERE ARE EACH BIRD'S CHARACTER VIRTUE STRENGTHS:

D-EAGLE CHILDREN love telling others what to do and like to be in charge of big picture tasks and problems to solve. **Assertive-**

ness, confidence, courage, determination and **independence** comes naturally to them.

I-PARROT CHILDREN seldom take on detailed tasks like their C Owl friends thrive in. They like to focus on people most often and their Character Virtue Strengths are **enthusiasm, optimism, trust, friendliness** and **generosity**.

S-DOVE CHILDREN do NOT like telling others what to do. They prefer setting up the systems that make life steady, more appealing and easier to function in. **Patience, loyalty, peacefulness, tolerance** and **cooperation** are the S Dove's Character Virtue Strengths.

C-OWL CHILDREN seem awed by how easily High I-Parrots can even talk to strangers and quickly make new friends. Owls prefer to focus on the details of a task and are also introverted. Their Character Virtue Strengths are **diligence, perseverance, perceptiveness** and **integrity**.

Initially, these qualities come from what you are taught as your family values and what defines the culture you belong to. But in every culture, there are universal **Character Virtues** that everyone has the capacity to exercise no matter what behavioral style you now find yourself using most often.

In saying that, some virtues are underdeveloped in each of the styles. D-Eagles find it difficult at times to practice patience as they have a fast pace and find slower-paced styles like the S-Dove rather frustrating, especially when it comes to S-Doves wanting to constantly steady the pace of their environment.

Here's a scenario a S-Dove mother shared with me about her teenage D-Eagle son. The mum says to her D-Eagle teenage son, "Darling, I'm heading to the supermarket and what would you like me to cook for dinner tonight? D-Eagle son says, "Mum, it's only 9 a.m. in the morning, it's a Sunday and I've just gotten up, do you think I know what I might feel like for dinner tonight now?" "Well, I know you've just gotten up," the mum says, "I was just trying to think of what you might like to eat tonight, that's all." Hmm, where might the conversation go from here?

It's all about having the desire to get a different result, gaining awareness of which virtue you seek, then knowing what language and behaviors to use that relate to it. **VOILA!** You've just shifted your style—and it no longer "has" you!

Finally, here are some strategies you can apply with examples for developing these virtues in yourself and in your children.

1. **FIND TEACHABLE MOMENTS WHERE A VIRTUE MIGHT BE NEEDED:** "Please be **kind** to your sister" or, "This is going to take some **patience** to complete" or "I need you to be **considerate** right now. Would you please turn down the volume?" With older children, you might say, "What virtue do you need to practice right now?" You can also use a virtue to acknowledge by saying, "Thank you for being responsible today, when you cleared up that misunderstanding with your sister."

2. **USE THE LANGUAGE OF THE VIRTUE:** Language has great influence to either empower or discourage someone or to build or not to build self-esteem. When you call a child stupid, bad or irresponsible and give a label to a certain behavior, then that is the behavior that follows. However, when you use words such as courage, responsible or respect that is also the behavior that follows, but in a much

more empowering way. Oh, and by the way, using the language of the virtues also works for adults too. Virtues also become a standard by which someone can bring themselves to being more accountable. Here's an example a teen might think to themselves, "Gosh, today I had some trouble with commitment, but I did take responsibility for cleaning my room when I got home." Always remember to be specific and accurate when acknowledging a virtue.

3. **SET CLEAR BOUNDARIES**: D-Eagle and C-Owl parents tend to constantly be in control mode. This can lead to a rebellious and unhappy child. Whereas I-Parrot parents tend to be less controlling and sometimes even practice no control at all, which can create a very unpredictable and chaotic environment for a child. It's all about you as a parent becoming the educator for your children—in the service of the child's learning.

Here are some guidelines for establishing family ground rules taken from Linda Kavelin Popov's book "The Family Virtues Guide." As a facilitator for the Virtues Project, we encourage parents to use these in their family's culture:

a. **BE MODERATE** – No more than five or six ground rules at any one time.

b. **BE SPECIFIC** – Create ground rules that meet the specific needs of your family.

c. **BE POSITIVE** – Avoid expressing rules using negative language.

d. **ESTABLISH SPECIFIC, RELEVANT CONSEQUENCES** – let the consequence fit the crime.

e. **BE CONSISTENT** – Children may test the limits especially those D-Eagle teenagers.

f. **COMMUNICATE RULES CLEARLY** – Write them up in a poster or on the fridge at eye level where a child can read them. You can even use humor.

g. **MAKE THE GROUND RULES NON-NEGOTIABLE** – The time for discussion is before the ground rules are established.

h. **REVISE THE RULES OVER TIME** – As children grow older or circumstances change, be willing to review the rules.

If you would like to find out what Bird Style you are or what style your children might be you can visit my website at **https://www.peoplesmartworld.com/store/p94/DISCkidsProfile.html** . Also, if you would like to learn more about the Four Primary DISC Styles, you can take my online self-paced course at PeopleSmart Academy called *"A Journey of Self DISCovery Level 1."* A DISC Assessment is included in the course **https://peoplesmartacademy.com/course/a-journey-of-self-discovery-level-1/**

My parting thoughts for you is to always believe that your kiddos can become confident, responsible, and respectful. It is your job to lead with empathy and understanding; the DISC Styles gives you a way to do that "By walking in another's shoes and understanding what they are experiencing." I hope I have inspired you to apply these strategies and tips with your children and the adults in your life. And as we say here in a PeopleSmart World,

---

"May all your relationships be filled with love and kindness."

RICHARD CHANDLER, MA, LPC

Dedicated to my past, present, and future clients and course participants, whose courage to face their lives and improve them inspires me.

ANGER & AGGRESSION

END THEM FOR A HEALTHIER YOU, COPARENT, AND KIDS

by *Richard Chandler, MA, LPC*

TUNE INTO YOUR BODY right now. Notice your level of relaxation. Stay aware for a half minute or so. Now ask yourself: "When was the last time I was upset, frustrated, and angry? Who was with me? What happened?" Replay the incident in your mind like a short film, from start to finish. Tune into your body once again and notice how it feels now. Did you feel muscle tightness, heat, or clenching? Where in your body? Racing thoughts or thoughts filled with swearing? Has your tension increased since tuning in the first time?

I'm here with you because, like you, I have acted out of anger and, in the aftermath, felt the pain of guilty remorse that follows. As a kid, I was on the receiving end of anger and aggression, which taught me to dish it out myself. It would have been better for me and those I raged at if my caregivers had the kind of education, insight, and skills practice you will receive in this chapter.

That is partly why I now specialize in working with anger in my private therapy practice and through my 8-hour **Transform**

Anger course. The other reason is that I have seen transformational results in clients who, despite decades of raging at their spouse, co-parent, and kids, embraced these ways of working with anger. Their outbursts ended and have not returned.

Their lives significantly improved, as did their mates' and kids' lives. That leads us to your anger, your co-parents, and the angry outbursts of your kids.

Could it be that your child's anger has more to do with you and your partner's example than your direct communication with them? By transforming anger—your co-parent and yours —your children will likely emulate your peaceful, healthy example.

Learn the following anger reduction skills for yourself. Teach them to your kids, primarily by example, and you won't live in the hypocrisy of "do as I say, not as I do."

Transforming anger is your opportunity to soothe the hurt your anger has caused and prevent the harm that will surely follow if you fail to take action on what you are about to read.

STOP TRAUMATIZING YOUR KIDS BY FIRST CALMING YOURS AND YOUR PARTNER'S ANGER

Parenting comes with a boatload of frustrations. Despite your intention to quit 'losing it', your anger pattern will repeat unless you learn to track and interrupt rising frustration levels. What path have your frustrations taken on their way to full-blown anger?

Even though it often happens quickly, frustrations build up to anger in a predictable pattern that can be discovered and interrupted by identifying "your unique anger pattern."

ANGER CONTROL: THE BOILING POT ON THE STOVE TOP ANALOGY

Anger control is like having a boiling pot with the heat turned on full and attempting to keep it from boiling over by putting a lid on it and leaning hard on that lid.

And just like holding down a cover on a pot of boiling soup, it will be even worse when it finally does boil over.

But there are better options.

1. You could take the boiling pot off the stove
2. You could keep it there and turn down the heat

THE FOUR HORSEMAN OF YOUR UNIQUE ANGER PATTERN

In my therapy practice, treating angry clients, and through my "Transform Anger" course, we'll start by discovering your unique anger pattern.

1. PUZZLED, RIGHTEOUS, AND "I'M THE VICTIM" THOUGHTS

Think back to the last time you got mad. Who was with you? What happened? Replay the scene. Next, answer these questions (in writing to gain the most from this process):

1. What were your thoughts at the time you became frustrated?
2. Did those thoughts contain some mix of puzzled, righteous, or "I'm the victim" words?
3. In what ways were your thoughts like these examples:
   a. "Why are they refusing to listen to what I've said?

b. "I don't get why they can't just do what I asked!"

c. "Why are they treating me this way? I deserve better!"

2. IDENTIFY EMOTIONS YOU FELT WHEN YOU BECAME ANGRY

Although anger is not your first emotion when frustrated, it may be the only one you can easily recognize. Usually, other feelings come first. For incidents of anger, have you also felt:

- Hurt?
- Embarrassment?
- Shame?
- Disgust?
- Sadness?
- Helplessness?

Those emotions are often more painful for you, your co-parent, and your children than anger. Instead of staying with those painful primary feelings, your emotions morphed into some degree of rage. Switching to offense allows you to escape more painful feelings than anger because "goddammit, I'm not going to take it!"

3. TUNE INTO YOUR PHYSICAL SENSATIONS AS ANGER ESCALATES

Your body is a reliable information source to know if you are in your unique anger pattern. Recall two or three separate incidents when you lost your cool. Please close your eyes if that helps and relive those incidents as if you are watching a movie. Slow down and press pause on your video to capture every physical sensation you can find.

What are you feeling physically at the very start of each incident? (You will likely have some but not all of the following.):

- Tightening or tension like winding up a spring? Where in your body?
- Heat or cold? Where?
- Some nausea, heaviness, or feeling of pressure? Where?

How do the above sensations spread through your body as you replay the incidents and your anger escalates? For many people, those sensations extend upward and outward. But not for all. For some, tension, heat, or cold starts from the hands, such as cold clenching fists, then travels through the arms into the chest, neck, and face.

4. BEHAVIORS OTHERS OBSERVE WHEN YOU GET MAD

As you replay your incidents, watch yourself from the viewpoint of those in the room. What would they see or hear?

- Fidgeting, animated gesturing, or pacing?
- Staring or looking away?
- Quieter or louder voice volume?
- A higher or lower pitched voice?
- Faster or slower-paced talking or yelling?
- More curse words or name-calling?
- Threatening gestures, hitting or throwing objects?

To ensure you covered them all, read your list to your co-parent and see if they can fill in any gaps. Consider that your behavior is what they experience from your angry outbursts. Is that how you want your mate and children to think of you?

BECOMING AWARE OF YOUR UNIQUE ANGER PATTERN SO YOU CAN INTERRUPT IT

Now that you know your unique anger pattern, you are in a position to interrupt it. Here is how. Ask yourself this question at random times, day or night: "Am I in the pattern?" Answer objectively:

1. SCAN your mind for thoughts you've identified with your anger pattern, including puzzled and righteous thoughts or thoughts of injustice with you as the victim.

2. NOTICE your mix of emotions, including anger, and assess their intensity.

3. TUNE into your physical sensations and notice how they have spread or intensified.

4. OBSERVE your behaviors as if from outside your body, witnessing them from another's perspective.

Frequently ask yourself, "am I in the pattern," then scan for indicators that you are. Doing so prepares you to automatically ask that question even when you only feel low frustration levels.

CHOOSE TO LEAVE IF YOU ARE IN YOUR ANGER PATTERN

Take the boiling pot off the burner. If, after asking, the answer is "Yes," choose to step away for a time. Leave so you can resolve things later after calming yourself since continuing could be counterproductive or might result in an angry outburst.

When your anger pattern is at an earlier stage, you might only leave for a few minutes. If it has already progressed farther along, as determined by your thoughts, emotions, sensations, and behaviors, perhaps you will need a half hour or longer to ground yourself and settle.

Stay as long as it takes to return to a calm state. But walking away does not mean you will not get back to discussing the matter at hand. Since you are the person who left, it is up to you to let your co-parent or kids know when you plan to be back.

And if you need a little more time, let them know within the time frame you said you would return. When back, if possible, do your best to complete the discussion where you left off.

ONE LAST THING: Let your co-parent, children, and teens know they are not to pursue you. Once you announce you are stepping out for a bit, their job is to drop the subject immediately, stay put, and not follow you.

CHOOSE TO STAY IF YOU ARE AT A LOW LEVEL OF THE PATTERN

Keep the pot on the stovetop, but turn down the heat. After asking the question, "Am I in the pattern," scanning and answering "yes," you can ask yourself a second question: "Is it at a low enough level that I can stay?"

You will only stay if you are less than a third of the way to full anger-escalation as judged by tuning into your thoughts, feelings, physical sensations, and behaviors.

DISCHARGE YOUR NERVOUS SYSTEM

We hold a charge in our nervous system like static electricity when stressed. Discharge it more subtly by shrugging your shoulders. If it isn't too inappropriate for the situation, it is even more effective if you gently jump up and down for a half minute or so while shaking your hands. By the way, kids love this!

When you do this for yourself, they will likely do it too, and everyone will feel more relaxed.

GROUND DOWN INTO YOUR HIPS, LEGS & FEET

Immediately bring all of your awareness to the lower part of your body, grounding into your hips, legs, and feet. Notice your lower body directly as a sensation; don't think about your body; notice it. As you do, frustration thoughts will automatically dissipate since your attention is no longer in your head but instead in your lower body.

If sitting, feel the pressure of your seat and the backs of your legs on the chair. Feel the warmth in your legs, feet, and hands as they rest on your upper legs.

LENGTHEN & DEEPEN YOUR BREATHING BY FOCUSING ON YOUR EXHALE

Here is the most effective way to enjoy relaxed, deeper breathing:

1. Where your exhale typically stops, gently squeeze out the rest of your air.
2. Relax for your inhale.

You will notice that your breathing naturally slows and deepens, and your inhalation will automatically be more extended and deeper by focusing on your exhale. Continue to focus on grounding down into your lower body and deep breathing, alternating between the two.

These discharging, grounding down, and deep breathing techniques work very well for calming whether you stay or use

DO THIS INSTEAD OF USING ANGER AND PUNISHMENT WHEN YOUR KIDS NEED CORRECTING

THE WISDOM AND EFFECTIVENESS OF "NATURAL CONSEQUENCES."

PUNISHMENT IS CONFUSING—because it comes from parents and caregivers who children believe are serving to love and protect them—and often is traumatizing. There is a better way; the skillful use of natural consequences.

Natural consequences flow directly and naturally out of your kids' behavior. They can understand and accept those consequences because they will see the direct connection between what they did or didn't do and those consequences.

Have you become angry when you have continued to remind your kids that they must gather their things and be ready so you can leave the house on time, only to have your children not do what you asked? Do this:

1. Purchase large clocks with hands that go around, one for each level of your home.

2. Point to the clock and say: "The clock says we have to pick up and gather our things so we can walk out the door when the hands get to here. That means you must begin getting ready to go when the hands are here and be finished by the time they are here. If we don't make it on time, the clock says there won't be enough time for us to _____." (Mention something fun for them.)

3. If they made it on time, follow through with the payout. If not, with no anger whatsoever, tell your kids that the clock couldn't allow the time to do the fun thing since they were not ready on time, but perhaps it will be different on another day.

Their behavior is bound to improve after a few instances of using natural consequences instead of yelling, guilting, or cajoling.

these methods to settle more quickly after you leave for your time out.

ANGER, AGGRESSION & PUNISHMENT

Aggression is related to anger, but unlike stand-alone anger, it is calculated, deliberate, and premeditated. Aggression punishes; when you use punishment, your example teaches your kids it is OK to set aside their humanity and treat people poorly or even hurt them.

You now have some core skills for recognizing your unique anger pattern and interrupting it by either walking away or staying by grounding down and deep breathing. Commit to practicing what you learned.

With their age in mind, teach your children and teenagers some of what you learned. But most importantly, show them by your words and actions that your days of yelling, indulging in angry outbursts, and dishing out punishment have ended.

Please get in touch with me with your feedback or questions. I'm curious to learn about your life and challenges and would like to be a resource for you.

Contact me:
PHONE: 320-223-9481
WEBSITE: https://relationshipscommunication.com
EMAIL: richardjchandler@gmail.com

PATRICE PORTER

*To my granddaughter who has had many adventures
in her garden and has experienced nature's
abundance through a bountiful garden!*

UNEARTHING LIFE LESSONS FOUND WHILE GARDENING

by *Patrice Porter*

TEN LESSONS GROWING IN YOUR GARDEN

These last couple of years where kids did a lot of online schooling and a lot of socializing online, it seemed that kids were getting hooked on their devices more and more, and some in unhealthy ways. Oftentimes, it is a real struggle to get them off their devices and away from their screens.

Why not give them an alternative that gets them out of cyberspace and brings them back into the natural world?

Give them an engaging activity where they'll learn a new skill that can serve them for a lifetime and one that is bursting with life lessons. I'm talking about opening the world of gardening to your children and let them become food producers for your family in the process.

Imagine the level of confidence and boost to their self-esteem if they become contributing members to the family food supply and how independence will grow with them through the process of gardening.

I often speak of life lessons that can come about from gardening; here are 10 of them:

1 AND 2 — Through gardening you can learn **RESPONSIBILITY**. To fully experience this, give your child ownership of their garden or a section of the family garden. Have them be involved right at the beginning stages with planning and all the way through by letting them do all that they are capable of. Their **decision-making** abilities will come into play here, too, as they choose things like where is the best place for a garden spot, deciding what they want to grow in their garden and where to put the plants or seeds.

3 — Starting a garden is a **COMMITMENT AND WILL NEED FOL-LOW THROUGH**. Do your child a favor and keep them on task by letting them blossom into full-fledged gardeners. You can give them a checklist of all the things to run through for the day or week to keep things in focus.

4 AND 5 — In the garden, kids will see there is such a thing as **CAUSE AND EFFECT** for plants are living things, and they need to be cared for and nourished because well cared for plants flourish and neglected plants wither and die. Let them see the consequences of their actions and learn what it is to have things dependent on them and learn **how to be dependable** in the process.

6 AND 7 — They will learn **PROBLEM SOLVING**. I like to have kids step back from their problem and look at it from all angles and perspectives. They should be encouraged to look at all the positive things they've done in their garden and use that positive feeling to take hold of their problems. This will enable them to more clearly define their problem and with that clarity, they'll find that it leads to solutions. Encourage children by asking in-

quiring questions about the problem and let the children do research for the solutions; this is very empowering. Through this
process they can **see their mistakes as opportunities to learn.**
Nature has many lessons to teach us, and it is full of wonders
with its infinite variabilities and patterns so it's important to
tune into nature. Get Mother Nature on your side, work within
her patterns and know she really wants your garden to thrive
and that those seeds that you plant are built to grow!

8 AND 9 — In gardening, you are shown **HOW TO LET GO AND
HOW TO DEAL WITH DISAPPOINTMENT.** For example—when you
have gotten to know your plants, their life cycles, and know
what they are capable of, then you'll know when things aren't
working, and you can let them go. In the process, you will learn
that things don't always work out, so you can use that lesson
for next time. Then, there are things that happen that are beyond your control—for instance, there may be hail, early frosts
or beloved pets may dig in the garden. Teach your kids to **persevere**, not to lose heart, and to keep planning, for their plans
are like a map for their journey and maps keep you moving in
the direction you want to go. Remember, there is always the
next growing season.

10 — An important lesson for this age with so much instant
gratification and feeling of entitlement is that of **PATIENCE AND
DELAYED GRATIFICATION.** Children need to learn that they must
earn things first and then they will be rewarded for their effort. We have our dreams of all the garden goodies but first, we
must plant our seeds, tend our plants, then we must wait. For-
tunately, those fresh, delicious fruits and vegetables are well
worth waiting for!

Let your kids experience and appreciate the abundance that
comes from the garden and hopefully they will have such abundance that they will have plenty to share with their friends and
neighbors.

HEALTH BENEFITS OF GARDENING

PHYSICALLY — Gardeners get vitamin D from being out in the sun, and they get exercise by toiling in the soil. And, by working in the fresh air, they sleep better.

MENTALLY — As a gardener's stress and anxiety are relieved through the act of gardening, they find more happiness and develop a type of mindfulness that is perfect when tending to their plants. There are studies that show working in the dirt releases the "happy" chemical serotonin, which boosts the mood.

EMOTIONALLY — Gardeners feel (and know) that they are a part of something, so they're not so alone. Plus, a more caring nature begins to develop from nurturing plants and the self-esteem is boosted as they contribute more.

INCREASE IN SPIRITUAL WELL BEING — Just being a part of nature does wonders for the spirit, and along the way, there are many lessons to be learned from nature.

Gardening is great for connecting with nature and it takes children out of cyberspace and into the natural world.

ACTIONS YOU CAN TAKE RIGHT NOW:

Take a moment from your busy life and think of what is important to you, and for your family.

With that in mind, look to places where you can shift things around or remove things so you can prioritize and find the time for what is important to you. Now you've got that straightened out, I want you to create a vision for your family life that will contain a goal. After that, hold that vision, set your intentions for the day, week, or month and have that vision drive your actions towards that goal.

I'd love to see your family come together in a loving and supportive way, being able to enjoy quality time together in something that is done away from your devices, something that is nature based. I'd love to see you create a family garden that is planned and built together, and in the process, you'll create some wonderful memories and enjoy the bounties of nature.

The first step is to let loose your imagination by starting to dream of what type of garden you would like. Then, find out what sort of garden your child would like.

You may dream of an abundant garden overflowing with garden goodies but your child may be wanting a place where they can have an adventure, perhaps a fairy garden. Food items can be part of a fairy garden too so create a forest of thyme or put in edible flowers. Maybe your child wants a quiet, secluded place where they can hang out. Sunflower forts are great for this and if you plant them in a circle, you'll create the walls of the fort. The sunflowers will grow quite tall and are adorned with beautiful flowers, which eventually will give a nutritional snack with their seeds.

For a teenager, to pique their interest, it may take growing some things that are cool and unique, things that are great conversation starters that can be shared with their friends. Giant vegetables like super-sized pumpkins, foot-long beans or uniquely colored vegetables like the ghost pumpkins (Lumina) which have a white skin and orange flesh and make great jack-o-lanterns. Purple carrots or unusual potatoes varieties are just some ideas. The sky really is the limit.

For planning what to put in your garden, take a trip to your local farmer's market and see what will grow in your area. Talk to other gardeners from your area. Let your child taste some of that fresh garden food and find out what foods your child likes to eat that they would be willing to put some effort in to grow them. Start planning out your garden and putting it down on paper – this effort starts making it real. This is also a good time to start a garden journal to record what you are doing and observing in your garden.

It's okay to dream big but in your plans, make it more like steppingstones to get you to the creation of your dream garden. Keep it small at first to prevent overwhelm for you can always expand later. I've created the "Gardening With Kids Playbook" which gives you the steps to create a garden all the way from choosing your garden spot to bringing in the harvest. Get a free copy at: **https://gardeninggrandma.co/gardeningbookgiveaway**

Take your time and enjoy your garden; it's a wonderful way to connect with nature. You'll find there is a lot going on in the garden so it's doubly important to give your kids time to explore. Help build their power of observation by encouraging them to ask questions. You may find while you are working together in the garden that all sorts of conversations can start up. Perhaps, as you're tending your piece of earth, it may bring about conversations about broader issues for caring for the environment.

Really take an interest in your child's gardening efforts and encourage them to talk about it, so take photos and keep the enthusiasm up. Those photos are great to put in the garden journal, and they are wonderful to refer to and see how much growth there has been. With keeping a garden journal or a simple photo journal, you can look back and reflect on what plants worked well for you and the things that didn't go so well that you may want to change for the next growing season.

May you be blessed with a bountiful garden full of lots of garden goodies!

Patrice brings lots of enthusiasm and creativity to her gardening projects and turns something that is often considered a chore into an adventure.

Kids can join in this gardening adventure with Patrice, A.K.A. the Gardening Grandma, in her "Got Dirt? Gardening for Kids" program found at: **https://thegardeninggrandma.com/gardening-for-kids.**

In addition, Patrice, with her *"Bright Futures Family Program"* works with families by offering support for parents to show up as their best self by being good role models for their children.

Patrice shows ways to disengage children from their devices and have fun doing healthy, meaningful activities. She encourages moving towards self-sufficiency, showing how a family can do more for themselves and prompting their kids in helping with gardening. Gardening is used as a family project, which helps tighten family bonds, all the while learning important life lessons that lead children towards growing to their greatest potential.

The *Bright Futures* program is geared to getting children on track to be well adjusted and have a bright future.

Patrice Porter is a mother, grandmother and avid gardener. She is a Certified Educational Associate and recently retired after 15 years working with young children in a "Play and Exploration program, something she absolutely loved. Patrice continues to work with children through her "Got Dirt? Gardening For Kids" program and "Bright Futures Family Program."

With a wealth of knowledge gathered through many years researching and training with renowned gardening experts, Patrice has become a sought-after gardening consultant who loves opening the world of gardening to folks, especially to children. Find out more at **TheGardeningGrandma.com** or consider booking a Discovery Call with her.

She loves the medium of books for sharing knowledge and expertise and is the author of the book series, "Bringing Out the Potential of Children." Find them and her other books on her author page at: **amazon.com/author/patriceporter**.

Patrice enjoys her peaceful life on her homestead in the Boreal forest along with the ability to connect worldwide in her online ventures. She believes gardening and growing your own food should be a part of every child's education, not only for the access to fresh, nutritional food that it gives but also all the other health benefits that can be achieved.

Patrice Porter

Contact me:
PHONE: (306) 469-5741
EMAIL: **patrice@thegardeninggrandma.com**
WEBSITE: **https://thegardeninggrandma.com**

NINA CRUZ

All of my greatest lessons & learnings could not have been possible without becoming a Mamma & birthing two of my greatest teachers. Jakob & Kira...thank you for waking me up in so many magical ways & for choosing me to be your Mamma. You are the greatest gifts I have received in this lifetime. I love you forevermore, Mama xx

CONSCIOUSLY CREATING YOUR EPIC MAMMA JOURNEY

by *Nina Cruz*

LIFE HAS A WAY of guiding us towards the path of our greatest growth, calling us to step up and live out our most authentic life. That being said, it is no coincidence that you are here and picked up this very book, nor that you called your child into the world. Your unique bundle of joy was divinely picked just for you!

"Change the way you look at things ... the things you look at change."
— DR WAYNE DYER

When I became a mother, my world literally changed overnight. I remember feeling profound love but also a great sense of responsibility. I had to get it 'right', I had to know it all, give my son the best of everything, be the best, do it all and not screw it up ... or him up! I felt this pressure to be the 'perfect' mother and not let my son down.

Little did I know at that time I would be embarking on the adventure of a lifetime, that my parenting would be the playground and sometimes battleground within which I would learn, grow, stumble, fall, pick myself up and ultimately be led to support others to do the same—navigate their own parenting journey with awareness, curiosity and a deeper connection to themselves and their child.

"We're all just walking each other home."
– RAM DASS

As you may have already realized, a child doesn't come with a manual. And often it can feel like we are fumbling our way around trying to figure it all out, and we can lose sight of the innate wisdom that resides inside us. We can feel pulled towards the outer world, feel stuck in comparison, and feel like every other Mamma is doing it right except us!

When I began to trust that I was 'more' than enough as a Mamma and that I was the exact Mamma my child needed, everything changed.

"It is never about what's going on outside of you
BUT what's going on inside of you."
– NINA CRUZ

YOUR CHILD IS TEACHING YOU

My children are my greatest teachers, and to think I thought I would be the one teaching them! What I didn't realize was that my own parenting journey would be a process of peeling away my own childhood conditioning, understanding myself better, discovering why I got triggered by something my child did or didn't do, letting go of all the stories I was playing out in my mind that I was not a good enough parent or didn't do enough or that there was something wrong with me.

I remember the first time I stumbled on Conscious Parenting and how it resonated deeply with me and started me thinking. Could it be me? Could the reason I felt challenged and overwhelmed as a parent be actually all about me, not my child?

Well, this was an epiphanic moment. My view and perceptions I had held that I needed to fix (blame), change, manage my child & my outside world—that they don't hear me, they don't listen—they fell to the ground, and I surrendered. I began to listen—listen to myself.

This moment shifted my parenting world and life forever. I couldn't turn back from here. I couldn't unlearn what I had learned. I could no longer blame my child—or anyone in fact. Ignorance is bliss! It was me, all me, and I had to look at what I was creating. Looking back, I am forever grateful for that moment.

"Conscious Parenting is about raising the child within us ... so we can raise the child before us."
— NINA CRUZ

Looking in the mirror isn't easy. There were parts I didn't like, sides of me where I was way too critical, focused on what was missing, couldn't enjoy the moment, was judgmental, wanted my children to behave and be good and be compliant.

You see, our mind is hardwired to look for what's missing and what's wrong. I had to learn to reprogram my mind and begin to shift my awareness and focus towards what I was grateful for and what I really wanted to create.

As I began to learn and grow, I saw patterns that had been playing out unconsciously since childhood, patterns where I would give my power away, letting the outside world dictate how I 'should' be, what I 'should' do, and I let life happen to me. I was constantly trying to control, fix, manage, improve and make others happy—make things better all on the outside so I could feel better on the inside. The outside world was steering my wheel and I was a passenger. And the impact of this was I sought to control my outside world. Little did I know my children would uncover how my need for control was getting in the way of the parent I desired to be.

"We are not living lives ... we are living patterns."
— DR SHEFALI TSABARY

YOUR CHILD IS YOUR AWAKENER

It was no coincidence I birthed two spirited and strong-willed children, who didn't want to fit into any kind of mould I may have desired in my 'fantasy child' world.

They had another plan for me. As I began to become aware of the patterns that were playing out, my thought patterns and my high expectations of what my child 'should' be doing—like sleeping all night long and having a daytime nap on my schedule—I realized how I was creating overwhelm and challenge for myself. I was setting myself up to feel like I was not doing it right, as I was looking outward not inward. I was letting the outside world control my inside world. My children were healthy and happy, yet my focus was on things that were out of my control.

My children are continually teaching me. They spotlight exactly where I need to grow and shine the light on where I need to loosen the reigns of control. If I embody an energy of control, they will meet me with resistance and disconnect from me.

They have also shown me that I cannot meet any of my own needs through them. They do not need to do things to please me (something I did growing up) and are free to express themselves and follow their own inner knowing, as I do my best to hold space for their own unique unfolding.

JOURNAL PROMPTS

What is your child teaching you? What is your child reflecting back to you ... about you?

What is your default mode when triggered? What do you do when you feel overwhelmed or challenged? What stories or beliefs do you hold about your yourself and your child that are not really true?

THE WISDOM OF PARENTING

When you become a Mamma, you literally birth a whole new way of life. A new world opens within you and all around you. Life as you know it will never be the same again. Not only will you continue to change, but your child will be changing and growing up before your eyes. Nothing stays the same, and your child will show you this. Inevitably, one day your child will leave the nest. So, the time you have together when your child is in their childhood is priceless!

In order to receive the gift of parenting, you must be open to the ebb and flow that goes hand in hand with being a Mamma, trusting the journey and staying true to your own Mamma wisdom, and remembering that there IS a gift in even the most challenging moments if you are open to seeing it, receiving it and surrendering to it.

MAMMA, YOU ARE HERE TO RISE

Your child holds the key to your own inner evolution. Your child is by far your greatest teacher. They are teaching you about you in every moment if you choose to listen, to answer the call, look in the mirror, get curious and see the treasures that lay within you and before you, in the chaos, the mess, the meltdowns and the mayhem of mothering, through the tears, the fears and the fatigue that you will experience and feel at times along this journey called parenting.

As a mother, you are called to higher states of acceptance and surrender than you may have ever experienced before. And this can be so challenging when you are sleep deprived and feel as if there is nothing left to give of yourself, let alone give back to yourself.

Your child is showing you exactly where you need to grow. In your interactions, they are mirroring where you need to let go and surrender, where you need to hold a boundary, where you need to be present and silent, where you need to speak up, discern, be compassionate, be playful, less rigid, less controlling, when you need to let go of expectations, of old beliefs and when you need to just relax and BE—be YOU and be with your child in the generous present moment.

YOU ARE THE PREDOMINANT CREATIVE FORCE IN YOUR PARENTING LIFE

I invite you to take this journey with me, a journey of unfolding into the grandest design of your own parenting journey. Yes, you get to create it! My intention is that the words you read awaken a knowing inside of you, filling you with new ideas and new feelings about your role as a Mamma, that you remember why you are here and why you were chosen to mother your child.

> "Your child is a pure reflection of you ... And it is in this remembrance of who you truly are ... That you can truly see them for who they are."
> – NINA CRUZ

To receive all the treasures bestowed upon you requires a letting go of how life 'should' be and how you think your child 'should' be. It requires you to see beyond what you see with your own two eyes. It requires you to listen not only with your ears but with your heart, seeing life happening for you and your child. Good, bad, right, wrong, ugly, pretty, chaos, calm, sleep, no sleep—it is all part of the journey that you have been called to as a Mamma.

> "If you do what you've always done, you will get what you've always gotten."
> – TONY ROBBINS

CREATING THE MAMMA YOU WANT TO BE RITUAL

In order to create the Mamma you desire to BE and the connection you desire to have with your child, you must look at where you are now and how you desire to BE.

1. What will you release and let go of that is standing in the way of YOU being the parent you desire to be? Write it all down now and release your old ways of thinking, doing, being and behaving. Let go of your 'fantasy' child – all the ways you think your child 'should' be or 'should' behave, all the ways you are not accepting your child for who it is they truly are. Then burn it. Burn the piece of paper. This will send out a powerful intention that you are ready to release the past and step into creating your own parenting journey.

2. Now write down how you want to BE as a Mamma and how you want to FEEL. How do you want your child to feel in your presence? What are you committed to? What kind of home do you want to create for your child? What kinds of things will you be doing with your child? Read this each morning to help you focus on your intention for the day. You have one shot at this sacred mission, and the more you hold this awareness in the forefront of your mind, the more you will step into your creation. You will BECOME it.

So how do you begin to consciously create the parent you want to be?

How do you shift from autopilot to conscious creator?

Here are eleven magical steps you can take to get into the driver's seat and steer your parenting journey and life experiences towards what you desire.

1. **ACKNOWLEDGE THAT YOU ARE THE CREATOR,** director, designer, artist, architect and curator of your life. That you are creating your own life experience.

2. **BECOME SELF-AWARE.** Awareness offers you the key to free yourself from automatic programs, patterns and habits that your subconscious mind is running on autopilot. Becoming self-aware will help you identify when you are NOT parenting from your wise Mamma self BUT instead parenting from your Inner Child that seeks to be seen, understood and validated by your child (your Inner Child is trying to meet your unmet needs of childhood through your child). This awareness will allow you to shift back into parenting from your wise Mamma and transform the dynamic between you and your child. Please refer to the diagram below.

Becoming Self Aware

ARE YOU PARENTING FROM YOUR WISE MAMMA SELF?
OR FROM YOUR INNER CHILD?

3. **UNDERSTAND THE POWER OF CHOICE:** you have a choice in each moment. If you make a choice that does not feel right, you have the power to choose again. You get to choose your mothering experience, you get to choose how you perceive it and how you create it, from the inside out.

4. **FOCUS MATTERS.** What you focus on you feel. What you focus on impacts your thoughts feeling and actions. Be aware of where your focus goes, and begin to flex this muscle of focus towards what you are really wanting to create in the moment.

Ask yourself...What are you focusing on & what is that focus creating for you? Our focus is creating our experience.

Please refer to the diagram below to see how you can explore what's going on in your thoughts, feelings & actions to deconstruct & disrupt the pattern loop.

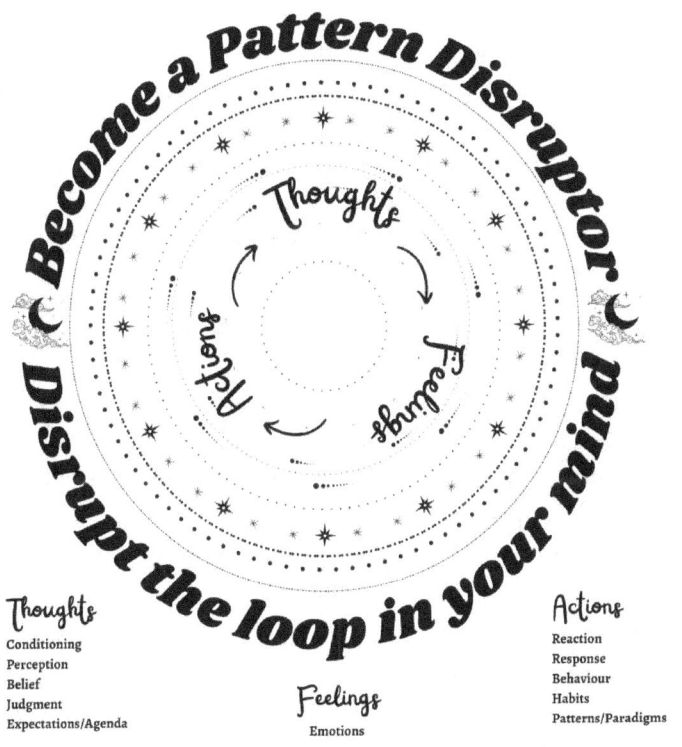

Thoughts
Conditioning
Perception
Belief
Judgment
Expectations/Agenda

Feelings
Emotions

Actions
Reaction
Response
Behaviour
Habits
Patterns/Paradigms

5. **DECIDE WHAT LENS YOU WANT TO SEE LIFE THROUGH.** Go within. Get curious. When you are triggered by something your child did or didn't do, turn the mirror on yourself. Remember, it is never about your child or anyone else. Ask yourself the following: What is the moment trying to teach me? What is this moment saying about me? What is my child teaching me? What is my child really needing from me? How do I need to show up in this moment?

6. **ACCEPT THE 'AS IS'.** Life is inherently neutral. Don't let the filters of good and bad, right and wrong, limiting beliefs, conditions, rules, expectations and judgments add meaning and keep you stuck in a mental loop. Begin to see life and your child as they are – their divine nature and essence. Connect to the truth of who they are beyond any behaviors you may be experiencing, choosing connection before correction. When you begin to see life 'as it is' you can detach from all the external chaos and come to the present moment without biases and without being charged or triggered. You show up empowered, without projection or judgment. This is freedom from within.

7. **FOLLOW YOUR TRUTH,** your north star, and have a clear vision. How do you want to feel as a parent? How do you want your child to feel in your presence? Get a clear vision of the parent you desire to be. Use your imagination and connect to how it feels. Then you embody this vision. YOU BECOME IT NOW. BE the parent YOU want to be NOW.

8. **CULTIVATE SELF-LOVE AND SELF-COMPASSION.** For me, self-care is about bringing love and tenderness to all the parts that make up you. Love yourself on the inside and it will be reflected on the outside. Feel your own feelings without judgment, and observe your inner critic with compassion – without letting it run the show! Embrace and love your inner child and meet her needs from within. You can't give what you don't have.

9. **DEAL WITH 'WHAT IS' NOT 'WHAT IF'.** This is the ultimate self-care tip. This can stop you going down rabbit holes in your mind and eliminate incessant worrying and anxiety.

10. **THE OUTSIDE IS A MIRROR OF THE INSIDE.** Your child is a mirror, reflecting back to you where you need to grow, shift, let go, surrender, flow and not control. What is your child reflecting back to you? About you?

11. **PLANT THE SEEDS YOU DESIRE TO GROW** in the garden of your mind, and nourish and nurture them daily. Yank out the weeds, and let go of what does not serve you or your child.

"There is no single effort more radical in
its potential for saving the world than a
transformation of the way we raise our children."
– MARIANNE WILLIAMSON

So, I will leave you with the final truth of parenting. Our time is limited.

We cannot go back or change the past; all we have is the present moment. It is a present we can give to ourselves and our child/ren and generations to come. When we can realize the importance of this very moment, and that we are creating it and have the power to sculpt it, we become the most powerful parents and creators in our life.

Your child is the manual! Follow their lead. Find the magic in the mayhem. And follow your own Mamma lioness guidance – it is fierce, and it is powerful.

You cannot get in the way of a caterpillar becoming a butterfly!

"People will forget what you said, people will forget what you did, but people will never forget how you made them feel."

— MAYA ANGELOU

Are you ready to dive deeper and begin to create the parent you truly want to be for your child? Connect and work with Nina, so you can be a part of the conscious parenting movement and benefit your child and your life in magical ways.

Connect with Nina:

WILD NETWORK CHANNEL: **http://bit.ly/NinaCruzCoach**

INSTAGRAM: **@ninacruzcoach**

FACEBOOK: **@ninacruzconsciouscoaching**
https://www.facebook.com/ ninacruzconsciouscoaching/

WEBSITE: **https://ninacruzconsciouscoaching.com/**

(to book your Free Discovery Session with Nina, go to her website) Download a free 12 Days of Presence Program: **https://ninacruzconsciouscoaching.com/free-offers/** — twelve days to become a more present parent.

Nina Cruz is a certified Conscious Parent Coach, Social Worker and Meditation Teacher who integrates eastern mindfulness with western psychology in helping parents heal their ancestral legacies. Her expertise has allowed her to collaborate with experts around the globe.

NELLIE HARDEN

I dedicate this work to the #happyhardens. "Us" will always be my greatest teacher in this life.

WHAT EVERY TEEN NEEDS AND HOW YOU CAN GIVE IT TO THEM

by *Nellie Harden*

I HAVE ALWAYS LOVED the idea, feel and beauty of a garden. Up close, some gardens are perfectly manicured with much manipulation, pruning, guiding and disciplined sheers. Some others grow quite wild without defined edges and barriers, sizes or shapes. When you pull the perspective back enough to envelop it all, you can see one collective, colorful, diverse, and chaotic (in all the best and worse ways) garden.

As the gardener, when you plant a lily, you can be fairly certain a lily will come of it. When you plant a daffodil, you can rest assured you will most likely see a daffodil. On the other hand, if you scatter the seeds of wildflowers, you will ride the roller coaster of surprise until you see what comes to fruition. It all depends on the intention.

Farming has never been an absolute guarantee of a crop though, has it? From the beginning of time, there has been the interference of the elements "out there," the players in the game that the farmer has no control over. A storm, a drought, an unwelcomed critter, a neighbor of cruel intent and so many other opportunistic divergences.

What can the farmer do? They step in, do the hard and do the best they can with the knowledge they have gained through generations past, their own experience and the new knowledge they collect in their journey.

Parenting is no different. We are all cultivating and building the beginning of someone else's life. It is no small feat. The exhaustion of preparation, planting, care, and the edge-of-our seat patience before the harvest of adulthood is all there.

Just like every plant requires sun, water, space, air, and nutrients ... Raising people also requires some elements that are essential to having a beautiful outcome in your garden no matter what you are trying to plant.

My name is Nellie Harden, and I am a family Life & Leadership Coach. I specifically take parents of teens and tweens on a journey. I first establish exactly where you are and then explore where you want to be by the time your parenthood/childhood experience expires at the end of (approximately) 6,570 days. Then, we build the map to get there together and begin the journey.

I am a lover and forever student of "the how" and "the why." I have studied science my entire life from the mechanics of biology and physics to the awe of processes and expression of psychology, habits, and disciplines. I have studied behavior from wild humpback whales in northern Australia, captive dolphins and belugas, domesticated dogs and cats, and I have spent the last decade plus in the messy kingdom of humans while developing a specialty in the, sometimes feral, world of teens and their parents.

We, as parents, have, what I call "Inevitable Impacts" on much of what is to come in our children's lives, which is, undoubtedly, both exciting and terrifying. But I believe in the family. I work in this corner of humanity because I believe the best way to change the world is through one living room at a time. Futures are being planted there and almost everything, and I mean E-V-E-R-Y-T-H-I-N-G, you do as an adult has roots back to your 6570 (those first 18 years of your life). The reflex behaviors, the first thoughts and the words that slip out never to be put back in. You are either working because of your 6570 or in spite of it.

Now, to be clear, we will always, always be a parent. That badge is as good as tattooed on our foreheads, but the vital role we play in cultivating our children during the 6570 looks different and demands a unique set of skills.

The five elements of growing (sun, water, nutrients, space and air) are bottom-line essential for every farmer and for any growing process to be successful, but the diversity of how this happens is as unique as every farmer itself and the same is for parenting.

There are five absolute essentials that any person needs to be successful, but before I get to those, I want to unwrap this "success" word a little bit.

Over time, this word, like so many others, has changed shape and perspective. But to be clear, when I say *"success"* I am not meaning white collar, corner office, or CEO success. I mean being a "Self-Disciplined Leader" in your life. This is the goal, right? They come into the world and are parent disciplined for the first half of childhood when we tell them exactly what to do, how to behave and react. Then, after "The Great Transition" of middle childhood, they are guided, disciplined and lead toward being a "Self-Disciplined Leader" ready to go out into the world equipped with a foundation of true confidence, real respect, growing wisdom and a host of mental wellness skill sets and mindsets. Being able to think, feel and behave in ways that create a positive impact on their, and others, social and mental well-being ... that is success, and it can take a million different forms!

OK, SO WHAT ARE THESE FIVE THINGS?

When I share these with you, they will seem familiar, and you will probably acknowledge that you have these same needs, and you do! But, just as the newly emerged seedling needs to feel those sun's rays the most and has an immense thirst for water, your children need these essentials in more desperate ways as a teen, especially today when social culture is moving in a herd mentality more than ever before.

TO BE SEEN

"The eyes are the window to the soul" is a saying that has origins from Shakespeare, ancient philosophers, Leonardo Da Vinci, the Bible and a host of other characters from throughout time.

There was a seemingly harmless joke going viral a while back where a family would put a blanket over a younger child, say 12 and under, and then take it off and pretend that child was invisible. The first couple of minutes were fun and games, but many times, this prank turned perilous as the child started truly panicking that no one could see them. Through their perspective, they were in the same place, with the same people, communicating even, but they were not being seen.

In the hustle and bustle of today, this scenario can easily go from the confines of a prank to the open reality of our lives. Your child walks into a room, not a single person looks up from their mind-consuming devices or their immediate task.

We are more connected than ever as a network of interests, game play, project collaboration, and seeming efficiency but it has come at the expense of being less connected as people.

In the second half of childhood, our children are silently screaming to be seen, noticed, and acknowledged. They change their appearance, their behavior, their words, their performance at school, sports and more to say, "Look at me! I am different. I am me. I am not sure who that is exactly yet, but I know I am. Just Look!"

Think about all the times when they were little and performing a new stunt or being creative in any way and what would they say? "Look at me!"

They still thirst for the same attention now. Someone to see them for who they are. To acknowledge when they walk into a room. To have eye contact with them. In the world, they are one of billions, but in your home, they are one of you.

TO BE HEARD

Much along the same lines as being seen, is being heard, except that we have a new element now and that is their evolving ideas and intellectual contribution.

Yes, they want to be seen and acknowledged that they are a person, but beyond that punctuated scope of glances is the idea that they are revolving out of the, "that's nice, honey" pat-on-the-head contributions to the conversations and decisions and into the "I have real thoughts, ideas and opinions" department in life where they can truly contribute.

If this train of "your thoughts matter" isn't caught during the teen years, it can lead to them finding somewhere, or someone else, where they can be heard and appreciated and drive a wedge of silence between you and/or lead to a life where they find it very difficult to voice an opinion and feel worthy of sharing. That, of course, grows into a life of consolation prizes and never being in the driver's seat of their own journey.

The most simple and beautiful gift you can give your child is to genuinely ask their opinion. Some of the greatest ideas, unencumbered by the many layers of life you carry, can come from your child. Perspectives you didn't even consider and ideas that lead to success. The sense of contribution they have from just being heard can give birth to more and more confidence every time.

Also, just because you ask and genuinely listen to their opinion, does not mean that you, as the family leader, will follow it every time. Just like in the "real world" out there, ideas are not always followed. Sometimes they are partially used or not used at all but giving them the space to share without the three villains of communication (interrupting, mocking and sarcasm) is the vital part in this essential human need that is amplified in the teen years.

If you listen to them, they are so much more inclined to listen to you.

TO BE LOVED

One of the greatest needs that has been recorded since the beginning of time. Love. In many ways, to know love is to know life.

Your child will hopefully know romantic love as they grow and mature, but that isn't the first love they can (and developmentally need to) experience. The first is love of family.

This is the love that guides and disciplines in a way that teaches them how to discipline themselves. This is a love that does not look like a power struggle, but more like "pull up a chair and let's talk." It's a love that reflects respect, kindness, compassion, and grace regularly.

One of the most precious and essential ways to express love with your child during these transition years is to apologize when you need to.

It sounds simple and somewhat contrary to the idea of love, seeing as you would have needed some conflict to have something to apologize for, but let me tell you this ... conflict will find you. I promise you it is not something you have to look for or create. In these years, conflict has a tracking beacon and will always be able to find you. The easy thing to do is give into the conflict. The harder, more necessary thing to do is to love through it.

Hard truth—You will not be perfect. Let's take that card off the table right now. You will not be and neither will they, BUT if you establish this mutual understanding of "un-perfectness" and set it on a firm foundation of love, then you will make it through even the biggest of teenage angsty waves.

If you are not perfect (and if you are human, this refers to you) then you are going to have reason to apologize at times and why is that important? Because an apology shows your child that they have permission to not be perfect too. It also displays accountability, understanding, forgiveness, grace, maturity, kindness, compassion, and respect. These are all things we want our children to use and practice and if we do not do it first, where are they to learn it from?

For them to love, they first need to be loved and in the teen years, to love through the trials can be one of the biggest obstacles a parent can face.

TO BELONG SOMEWHERE

I recently went on college tours with my oldest daughter and most of these campuses have 300-400 clubs for their students. The saying was, "We have so many places for you to find your people and if you can't, then make a new club!"

This right here is a double-edged sword sign of our world today. You have so many places you can belong, but nowhere you feel like you do belong.

If you are standing in the middle of a courtyard with 400 people around you screaming your name, it is hard to tell if they are screaming for you or against you. This is what many of our teens can feel like today through social media, school, college campuses etc. You end up a crumpled mess on the ground covering your ears, alone.

The only solution is to quiet the voices and sort through to find your interests. Remember those farmers we talked about before? A plant has one main stem and then many branches, right? You can think of the main branch as your home and family where they first (and always) belong and everything else as the tree of life they are growing with interests and activities branching out in every way.

If they do not have that first place where they belong, their interests have nothing to grow from that produces real fruit and can truly grow.

How can you help them feel like they belong though? Isn't that just a given because you have paid for their trombone lessons, soccer uniforms, food, and braces for the last decade plus and given them a roof over their head? No. That isn't belonging. That is just a physical space, a dot on a map, not true belonging.

You want to include them in the home (not the house, the home). Honor the role they play in the everyday and let them really know how much they are needed and wanted. From the stairs being swept down to the dinner table conversations and their opinion you could really use. The sisterly help that only they can provide and their part in the teamwork a project requires.

Give them a place to know what true belonging feels like, so they can go out into the world and find more of it for themselves.

TO HAVE A PURPOSE

You can think of purpose like a compass. Life is constantly moving ... constantly. My father passed away when I was a young child, but he was in a coma for nine months before he died. Even while he was resting for all those months, life was moving in him and around him.

Do you know what it is called if you are in a forest constantly moving, but not knowing where you are going? You are lost.

What does this mystical life compass look like? It looks like them researching interests and setting goals. It looks like you partnering with them to explore interests together to create a common stage you can both play on. It looks like talking about tomorrow and what they need to do today in order to make that happen or avoid something else.

There is no such thing as standing still in life. You can find stillness, in fact, I recommend we all practice this to help achieve our purposes, but this is stillness in the journey. The journey never stops.

Always having a purpose, no matter how great or how small, is one of the absolute yearnings of every life.

In parenting teens, these five needs remain foundational and added to this is helping them build value and appreciation of self (aka self-esteem) and then further leading them toward that Self-Disciplined Leadership so they can go out into the world equipped to bravely live out their unique story. This requires communication, perspective, resilience, and discipline— skills uniquely crafted to your family.

You can't protect them against everything, or see everything coming, but you can be like the farmer and use your generational knowledge, experiential knowledge and seek out new knowledge to raise your crop the best it can be. You can give them the elements and the space to grow, the light, the water, and the air. Even in the more challenging phases of teen life, you can be there to help guide their roots and grow their first branches into life.

To learn more about the practical and simple things you can do at home to give your child these five essential needs, please go to **www.nellieharden.com/5needs.**

We have approximately 6,570 days before the harvest of this childhood/parenthood journey and every day is a part of their growth.

Other places we can connect:

https://linktr.ee/nellieharden

FACEBOOK: Family Architect's Club (parenting community for parents of teens and tween young women)

WEBSITE: **www.nellieharden.com**

INSTAGRAM: **@nellieharden**

"Ignite Her Joy Parenting Workshop: Building Your Daughter's Mental Wellness In Her Tween & Teen Years" (for parents of teen and tween young women) **www.nellieharden.com/ignite**

Podcast "The 6570 Family Project"(for all parents of tweens and teens)

MICHELE BENYO

This chapter is lovingly dedicated to my children,
the lights of my life, my heroes and wisest teachers,
David and Deanna, forever siblings by heart

GIVE YOUR CHILD THE GIFT OF GOOD GRIEF

by *Michele Benyo,*
CGRS, MEd, Founder of Good Grief Parenting

UNPLANNED-FOR EXPERIENCES change the trajectory of our lives in unimagined ways. So it is that this northern Minnesota small-town girl is a mentor to parents whose grief journey is familiar to me, and a voice for the youngest of grievers. I can chart footsteps throughout my life that led me here even before my precious 6-year-old son died of cancer.

And before his little sister said to me, "Mommy, half of me is gone."

One encounter at a time, the future I saw for myself shifted from one exciting occupation to the next—from becoming a high school English teacher out of college, to serving as a public affairs officer in the Army National Guard, directing communications for suburban school districts and non-profits—and, ultimately, becoming a mom. That changed everything and is the most cherished role I could ever have. My heart's desire ever since has been to hold gently the wonder and well-being of children.

The best way to care for children is to support the parents who love them. When my son was three and I was pregnant with my second child, I went back to school to earn an early childhood parent educator license and my masters in Family Education.

In one class, I was introduced to the concept of "loss of dreams." It made a deep impression on me—the fragility of dreams and how quickly a family's expected happy trajectory can be derailed. I decided then that I would be there for families who lose their dreams.

Little did I know that I would soon lose mine.

Just a few months into my early childhood career, I learned that my 4-year-old son had cancer. His sister was 15 months old. They were mutually adoring siblings. I had my dream job. Our life was perfect, and then it wasn't.

My son battled cancer for two and a half years. My daughter was three-and-a-half years old when her beloved big brother, best friend, and only sibling died. The loss was excruciating. It broke our hearts and left an unfillable void in her young being.

As devastating as it was for me, I felt my daughter's loss even more deeply than my own. None of my training had prepared me for this. No one could tell me how I was supposed to parent my daughter who said to me, "Mommy, half of me is gone."

I found few resources to help me navigate our unthinkable new reality. My daughter's whole lifetime lay ahead of her; her healing and wholeness were non-negotiable. I would figure it out on my own. And I knew I would have to share with other parents what I learned and discovered along the way.

What I learned over the next 20 years about grief—particularly children's grief and early childhood sibling loss—resilience, and parenting while grieving after child loss, has become the foundation of my *Good Grief Parenting* approach.

Childhood sibling loss has deep ramifications that few people recognize; it impacts the most basic of day-to-day interactions. My daughter spoke it so well one day on the playground a few years after her brother died when she said to me, "No one can know the pain that we feel." She is now a young adult, and the statement is still true.

As a Certified Grief Recovery Specialist™ and an early childhood parent mentor and coach, I come alongside parents who are grieving the death of a child and are faced with parenting their young bereaved siblings. I offer guidance, encouragement, tools, and hope that give them the confidence to thrive in the presence of grief and to live forward toward bright possibilities and even joy.

Author Anne Roiphe calls this "the remaking of life." She wrote, "Grief is in two parts. The first part is loss. The second is the remaking of life."

"Grief is in two parts. The first part is loss.
The second is the remaking of life."
—ANNE ROIPHE

The *Good Grief Parenting* approach provides sound guidance, parenting practices, and tools for any adult who wants to support young children grieving a loss of any kind. It aligns closely with the three steps of Jaci Finneman's *No-Problem Parenting*™.

STEP 1: SEEK FIRST TO UNDERSTAND

Many adults never learned helpful ways to cope with grief. When a child is grieving, they default to what they learned, and in most cases those responses are not helpful. Before an adult can help a child grieve well, they need to understand two things—the truth about grief and how children experience it.

THE TRUTH ABOUT GRIEF

Grief is the normal and natural human response to loss of any kind, and it's necessary for healing. No matter how painful, going right through grief is how we heal. In the process, we learn life skills to cope with loss. Grief is good. Children don't need to be protected from grief; they need to be supported through it.

Six common grief myths identified by The Grief Recovery Institute often get in the way of healing. Each myth can be reframed into a truth about grief that is foundational for the *Good Grief Parenting* approach.

- **DON'T FEEL BAD.** *Truth:* **IT'S NORMAL, NATURAL, AND OKAY TO FEEL BAD.** Rather than try to distract or cheer up a child who is grieving, acknowledge their pain. They don't have to "feel better."

- **REPLACE THE LOSS.** *Truth:* **GRIEF CAN'T BE FIXED.** Each loss is unique and needs to be honored. When a child is grieving the loss of something or someone, it's not helpful to suggest getting a new one to replace what is lost.

- **KEEP BUSY.** *Truth:* **GRIEF CAN'T BE AVOIDED.** Feel grief and it to heal. Children don't need activities, treats, and busy-ness when they're grieving; they need routine, consistency, and familiar space to just be.

- **BE STRONG.** *Truth:* **GRIEF IS NOT WEAKNESS.** You don't have to be strong. It's okay to cry; tears heal. When we allow children to see our grief, we are teaching them that grief is an appropriate and acceptable response to loss.

- **GRIEVE ALONE.** *Truth:* **SHARING GRIEF HEALS.** Grievers appreciate a caring presence. Nothing you can say or do will take away your child's pain, but quietly caring, being accessible, and listening offer comfort.

- **TIME HEALS GRIEF.** *Truth:* **ACTIONS AND CHOICES OVER TIME ARE WHAT HEAL GRIEF.** There is no set timeframe for healing, but simply waiting will not heal grief. Healing is a choice supported by intentions—and small action steps.

HOW CHILDREN EXPERIENCE GRIEF

Young children don't understand the concept of death, but they respond to the absence of their loved one and the reactions of others around them. They feel grief, although they don't understand it.

Like adults, children can have a variety of grief feelings in response to a loss.

- They may feel sadness, a deep sense of sorrow, or loneliness, and will miss the person who died.

- They may feel anger about the death of the person and have a feeling of powerlessness.

- They feel fear, confusion, and uncertainty. Their world has been shaken.

- They may feel responsible and guilty, even when it isn't reasonable. Young children believe that thoughts cause actions and may feel responsible for what's taken place because of something they thought or did.

CHILDREN'S GRIEF RESPONSES VARY WIDELY.

- Some act younger or regress, resorting to whining, thumb sucking, and even wetting their pants. They want the care and attention they received when they were younger.

- Others become over-achievers to compensate for their feelings of helplessness. They try to do everything "right" to avoid upsetting their parents.

- Others become aggressive to counteract the vulnerability they feel. These emotions expressed as angry outbursts or misbehavior may not be recognized as grief related.

- Others withdraw and become very quiet, feeling fearful and insecure.

- Fears and insecurity may show up as anxiety, nightmares, or physical symptoms (aches, pains, sleep disturbances).

- Children grieve in spurts, as they are not able to tolerate the intensity of grief for prolonged periods of time.

- Children often cope with grief and loss through play, which is their natural way of processing experiences. Adults often leave children alone when they're playing rather than engage them, not realizing it could be helpful for the child to talk about what they're playing and feeling.

Grieving children need your reassurance and loving arms. They need you to recognize their grief, to avoid punishing or shaming them for challenging behaviors, and to provide acceptable ways for them to express their feelings.

STEP 2: PREPARE FOR THE WORST

Childhood is the best time to learn about loss and grief, just as it is the best time to learn many other skills and truths about life. *Good Grief Parenting* gives parents effective ways to build children's resilience and equip them to manage inevitable losses and life challenges. Two tools are essential messages and teachable moments.

ESSENTIAL MESSAGES

Every child needs to receive critical life messages that help them feel loved, build their self-esteem, and equip them to be powerful in their world. This is especially true in stressful times. When parents are intentional about giving their child essential messages through both words and interactions, they reinforce a child's resilience and sense of well-being. For example:

When a child's **sense of security is shaken** by the death of a sibling, they need to know:

I love you.

You are important to me.

Your feelings matter.

I am here for you.

You are safe with me.

When a child **encounters adversity or hardship**, they need to know:

I know you can handle this.

You can learn how to help yourself.

You can have help if you need it.

You will get through this.

We will get through this together.

When a child **exhibits challenging behaviors**, they need to know:

Big feelings are difficult to manage.

You matter, and your feelings matter.

You can learn appropriate ways to express big feelings.

I understand this is hard for you.

I am here for you.

TEACHABLE MOMENTS

A moment in an ordinary day can provide an opportunity to teach your child about life, death, loss, or grief. A teachable moment may arise in a chance encounter such as finding a dead bird on the playground, or a circumstance such as being sad because their hamster died. Use the opportunity to talk with your child, and to hear what they're thinking and feeling and what they wonder about.

You can plan a teachable moment using a book, special activity, or field trip to provide a context for a conversation. Every teachable moment prepares your child to deal with grief when it comes into their life, as it inevitably will.

STEP 3: CHANGE THE CONVERSATION

When a family encounters loss and grief, often an adult's instinct is to shield a child from the painful reality. They may not talk about it with or around the child, or they may deny what is really happening, say it's nothing to worry about, or somehow soften the truth.

Children feel what is happening in the family; they sense that something is not right. *Good Grief Parenting* gives parents three keys to change the conversation with young children when it comes to grief—be honest, talk about it, and connect with your child.

BE HONEST

Although young children don't understand the concept of death, they still should be told the truth with words that accurately tell them what happened. Tell them that the person died and is dead (not went to sleep or went away, passed, or is sleeping, gone, or lost). Explain that when a person dies their body stops working. They can't do the things they used to be able to do. They can't talk or eat or play or laugh, and we won't see them anymore.

Provide honest, factual, age-appropriate information about what happened without a lot of detail. Answer their questions simply.

Avoid telling a child something untrue to soften the truth.

TALK ABOUT IT

Let your child know when you are feeling sad or other emotions that can be part of grief. Speak it, name it, normalize it. Ask if they feel that way, too. Do they want to talk about it? Is there anything they wonder about?

Invite them to talk, but let them know it's okay if they don't. You are making it okay to talk about grief and other difficult things when they need to.

CONNECT WITH YOUR CHILD

Young children are trying to make sense of feelings they can't understand. Validate what they're feeling and let them feel it. Listen to them without trying to fix it. Give hugs.

Too often, well-meaning adults try to distract children from uncomfortable feelings or try to cheer them up. This doesn't work with grief, and it's not helpful. Grief educator Earl Grollman tells us, "The only cure for grief is to grieve."

"The only cure for grief is to grieve."

—EARL GROLLMAN

Find specific suggestions for changing the conversation about grief in my Good Grief Guide. Get the free download at **https://goodgriefparenting.com/ggg**

GOOD GRIEF PARENTING equips parents and other caring adults with the accurate information, skills, and tools to support grieving children through what they're experiencing. Children who are supported through grief in helpful, healthy ways grow up to be adults who can talk openly about grief and support others through it.

Children who are given the gift of good grief will literally change the world!

Parents that I work with gain an empowered and hopeful outlook so that they can enjoy life again after the death of a child and can help their young children grow up whole and happy.

I offer trainings and workshops to give other caring adults the good grief essentials they need to support young children who are grieving.

When children and families are supported in healthy grieving, they can live forward after loss toward a future bright with possibilities and even joy. **This is my hope!**

Find good grief resources and connect with me:

VISIT: linktr.ee/goodgriefparenting

THE GOOD GRIEF GUIDE: https://goodgriefparenting.com/ggg

WEBSITE: www.goodgriefparenting.com

EMAIL: michele@michelebenyo.com

MELISSA DEALLY

I'd like to dedicate this chapter to Janice O'Mara
for setting me on the right path and to both my
daughters, Nicole and Samantha who have taught me
so much and helped guide me into the work that I'm
so passionate about today!
Thank you all!

HOW NUTRITION IMPACTS YOUR CHILD'S LEARNING AND BEHAVIOR

by *Melissa Deally*

A LOT OF PEOPLE don't realize there is a connection between the food our children eat and their ability to thrive in school, or their behavior. Even less understood is the impact nutrient deficiencies and toxins can have on our kid's overall health. So, I'm very happy you are here, wanting to learn this, as once you know this information, you can take very simple steps to achieve some profound results for your kids and for yourself without the need for a daily dose of pharmaceutical drugs.

First, let me introduce myself and share my story. My name is Melissa Deally, and I'm an Integrative Mind Body Health Practitioner. I'm also trained in Neurolinguistic Programming (NLP), Timeline Therapy and Hypnotherapy. However, when my daughters were in elementary school, I was in the corporate world and didn't have the knowledge I have today about health and nutrition. I am eternally grateful to my oldest daughter's 2nd grade teacher, Mrs. O'Mara, as she pointed me in the right direction and saved us a lot of time figuring everything out on our own, and so now I'm doing the same for you.

When Nicole was at the end of 2nd grade, I was picking her up after school one day and Mrs. O'Mara said to me, "I'm concerned about Nicole as I've noticed that her handwriting has regressed this school year, and she is less able to sit still and focus than she was at the beginning of the year." I felt a bit dumbfounded by this information, and as I helped Nicole pack up her backpack, all I could think was, "I have no idea how to help Nicole with this." So, I turned back and asked the teacher, "How do I support Nicole over the summer, so this improves?" Mrs. O'Mara said, "It could be food, you might want to check into that." To which I responded with "How do I do that?" not having a clue as to how I'm supposed to check a correlation between food and her handwriting or ability to focus. She said, "You might like to get some food testing done with a naturopathic doctor, I've just done it myself, it might provide some answers."

Wow, I didn't even know that kind of testing was available, but I already worked with a naturopath myself, so I contacted her and asked about this food testing. What we learned from that lab test was eye opening! It turned out Nicole was sensitive to both sugar and yeast.

Once I knew that, I was able to remove them from her diet and within a few weeks, I saw a marked difference in her behavior. Gone were the meltdowns, especially the ones with her crying "I don't know why I'm crying Mommy" because her body wasn't able to process the sugars / yeast, it was leaving her feeling "out of control" and between that and the insulin crashes, she would have a meltdown nearly every day, but not even know why. Because I was used to that behavior from her, I just thought it was Nicole being Nicole and never thought to look at her diet.

When she returned to school that fall, she was in Mrs. O'Mara's classroom again for the first week and on Friday, Mrs. O'Mara told me that she was a different child compared to June, she could sit and quietly focus, her handwriting was much improved and "look how many pages she wrote about her summer holiday!!"

Three years later when my younger daughter, Samantha, was in the 1st grade, her teacher told me she'd been complaining of tummy aches after lunch and would just sit with her head on her desk for the rest of the afternoon every day that week. I'd also noticed her choosing not to go on playdates after school, and she didn't want to play soccer either (her favorite sport!). I took her to the doctor only to be told "all little girls get tummy aches, she'll grow out of it," but received no indication as to how long that would take.

She was miserable, and I wasn't willing to accept this, so I emailed the naturopath, explained the situation and asked if she thought food testing could help and she said "Yes!" We did the same lab tests again, and this time we learned that Samantha was sensitive to gluten and dairy. Good to know, seeing as I'd been feeding her both on a daily basis, sometimes twice a day, as I had no idea that she was sensitive to them. So, I changed her diet and inside two weeks, she was back to her happy, social self, playing soccer, going to playdates, and she was fully participating at school again. It was so helpful to be able to run these lab tests and get the information needed to support the girls so they could get back to thriving.

My career has changed since those days, and now I offer that same food sensitivity lab test to my clients. Working with me means we stop guessing and start testing so we can clearly understand the child's food sensitivities, nutrient deficiencies, metal toxicities and/or gut health issues—all of which can impact how they feel, behave, and learn.

We use lab testing to seek to understand what is going on. Where are the deficiencies and imbalances in the child's body that are causing behavioral or learning issues or both? Once we know this information, we then know exactly what foods or toxins to remove, what nutrients to add to their diet, or how to rebalance their gut. It saves a lot of time guessing, as when we know how to support their body, the body responds very quickly because we are providing what it needs.

You're probably thinking that this is too good to be true, you didn't know it could be this easy right? Well, it literally can be, until your child refuses to co-operate with their new meal plan. Obviously, the age of your child matters, as the younger they are, the more control you have over their food and the less likely they are sourcing their own food. The older the child, the more ability you have to communicate with them so they start to connect the dots between how they are feeling and the food they are eating and how much better they feel when certain foods are removed.

The foods don't have to be removed forever. I'm not talking about anaphylactic allergies here. I'm talking about food sensitivities, nutrient deficiencies, candida or yeast overgrowth. There is a difference, this isn't a life, or death situation, and so the dietary changes don't have to be implemented forever, typically a 3-month window is enough time for healing to take place, and then foods can be re-introduced and enjoyed infrequently (not daily), but perhaps weekly or monthly, depending on how their body responds.

To a child I know three months can feel like forever, and not getting to eat the same food as their friends can be problematic, but it can be done. It took more work on my part, but I talked to my girls about what was really important to them and what they could live without. Here are some of the changes we made:

- School pizza day – the pizza company was able to make a pizza on a yeast free dough for Nicole – I paid extra for this, but she still got her pizza like the other kids

- If they went to birthday parties, they also took their own homemade cupcake instead of eating the actual birthday cake. They knew their own cupcakes didn't give them a tummy ache!

- Breakfast became fruit with a gluten-free English muffin or homemade apple muffin or fruit smoothies made with almond milk.

- Lunch was no longer sandwiches, and instead was soups, salads, dinner leftovers, as well as scones made from spelt flour. The lab test showed Samantha was okay to eat spelt flour, as well as some cheeses, just not dairy milk.

- After school snacks were often peanut butter on gluten-free crackers with some fruit or veggies and dip.

- Dinner was easy to serve with no gluten, sugar, dairy or yeast. We used rice or rice pasta, lots of veggies and fish or chicken.

These are some of things that we did, there are many more things you can do, but what's important is getting your child involved by asking them for their ideas on what they can eat to feel better. If you tell them what they 'have' to eat, they will likely refuse it. You also need to let them fall and learn for themselves. They might eat well for a while and then decide they're going to eat whatever they want. Don't be angry, be there to support them when they aren't feeling great later. This isn't a place for "I told you so," instead it's a chance to ask a question like "What is your body trying to tell you right now?"

This is such a great opportunity to teach your children the lifelong skill of listening to their body. Let them know their body talks to them in the form of "symptoms" and so if they eat something and don't feel good, that is their body asking them not to eat it. Let them know that their body will always guide them in how it would like to be fed. As they learn this, they will be able to make better choices for themselves.

Symptoms of "not feeling good" from food may manifest as your child feeling overly excited, feeling out of control, having a temper tantrum, feeling really tired, unable to stay awake in class, feeling jittery, can't sit still, unable to pay attention, or even a tummy ache or skin rash. A gluten sensitivity will often trigger this type of behaviour as their little body struggles to process the glutamate in it; this is an excitatory neurotransmitter and is the same as MSG.

This is also a great time to start teaching your kids that they need to take responsibility for their own health, and that there are natural protocols that can be considered in most cases in deciding a course of action. A medical doctor is trained to write prescriptions, but they are not trained in nutrition, digestion and lifestyle factors that impact our health. Working with someone who is trained in these areas can result in a great partnership where you can get the answers you're looking for plus support along the way, so you don't feel alone navigating this path.

Kids also learn from modelling your behavior. How healthy are you feeling? What choices do you make around food? If you are changing your child's diet, change your own too, so they can see you are doing this with them. If you improve your own nutrition, you will find you gain energy and feel better as a result too.

What action steps can you take now?

Start by having your child drink more water. Sounds simple I know, but too many kids are living on fruit juice (loaded with sugar – yes, natural sugar, but without the fiber from the fruit, it's too much sugar. A juice box of apple juice has 28g of sugar in it – that's 7 teaspoons!) Would you let your child eat 7 tsp. of sugar? Ditch the energy drinks (loaded with sugar and food coloring) as well as pop (loaded with sugar and other chemicals) and get them enjoying water, which will hydrate their body properly. An extra tip: Room temperature drinks are more hydrating to the body than chilled drinks.

Hang the "poop chart" (see next page) in your bathroom and teach your kids what healthy poop looks like. This way they can let you know when their poop isn't healthy, as that is a clue to something going on in their gut – perhaps they haven't had enough water! They'll be able to self-correct before too long using this chart!

You can also start removing dairy and gluten, the two most common trigger foods and track their behavior while keeping a food diary. Although, it is much easier to run the lab tests as I did and then know exactly what foods to remove. There are several labs tests that can be helpful in understanding the root cause of a child's learning or behavioral issues:

- Complete Food Sensitivity Lab Test (food assessment)
- Complete Candida, Metabolic and Vitamins Test (gut health assessment)
- Complete Metals & Minerals Test (assesses metal toxicities and mineral deficiencies)

In today's world, even our babies are being born toxic and deficient. Check out Environmental Working Group's (**EWG.org**) documentary called "10 Americans" (**https://www.youtube. com/watch?v=0-kc3AIM_LU**). If mom has toxins in her body during the pregnancy, they can pass through the placenta, and if she is deficient in vitamins and minerals, then baby is born deficient too.

How Well Do You Know Your Poop

Shapes of poop

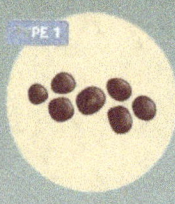

TYPE 1

Marbles
Indicates: These little pellets typically mean you're constipated. Eat more fiber and drink more fluids.

TYPE 2

Lumpy Log
Indicates: This is still a sign of constipation, focus on improving hydration and eat more fruit & veggies.

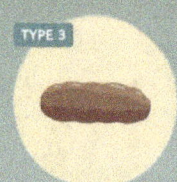

TYPE 3

Log-shaped with so[me] cracks on the surfac[e]
Indicates: This represents healthy poop, but the crac[ks] indicate your body still nee[ds] more water.

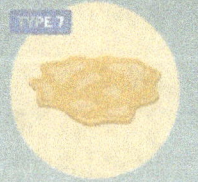

TYPE 7

Watery with no solid pieces
Indicates: In other words, you've got the runs, or diarrhea. Your body is likely fighting an infection, drink electrolyte infused beverages to ensure you don't become dehydrated.

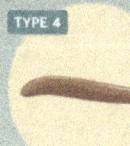

TYPE 4

Sausage or a S[...]
Indicates: This is th[e] form of poop! Your [...] doing fine!

TYPE 6

Fluffy and mushy with ragged edges.
Indicates: This too-soft consistency could be a sign of mild diarrhea. Try adding electrolyte-infused beverages to help improve this.

TYPE 5

Amoebas
Indicates: These blobs have clear cut edges and are normal if pooping several times per day.

OWN: You're fine. Poop naturally brown like the our of cardboard.

GREEN: Have you eaten lots of green leafy veggies, or green food coloring? If not, this could be a sign that food may be moving through your large intestine too quickly.

YELLOW: Greasy, foul-smelling yellow poop indicates excess fat, which could be due to poor absorption of fat in your digestive tract.

K: Some vitamins aining iron or bismuth alicylate could cause poop. It could mean you are bleeding nally due to an ulcer or er. Pay attention if it's y, and see your doctor 're worried.

RED: Blood in your poop is never a good sign and warrants seeing your doctor for further testing.

WHITE: Light coloured, white, or clay coloured. This could be due to some medications or could mean a bile duct obstruction. See your doctor about this.

How often should you poop?
On average, people go once or twice a day but some may go more and some may go less. As long as it's not daily constipation or daily diarrhea, and you feel comfortable, you're fine!

How keep your poop healthy?
- Eat a diet high in fiber (20-25g), drink lots of water and get regular exercise, which help keep everything moving well.
- If you're having trouble pooping (constipation), dietary fiber can help make the passage smoother.
- Proper hydration helps ensure your colon is slippery enough for the poop to move through.

When to see a Doctor?
Don't panic the first time you see something out of the ordinary in your poop. See if it happens again. If symptoms persist, then go talk to your doctor. Pay attention to what you body is telling you, and whenever you feel uneasy, it's time to go see your doctor.

Quick facts about poop

 The food you eat usually takes 1 - 3 days from the time you eat it until it ends up in your poop.

 Poop is made up of undigested food, bacteria, mucus, and dead cells, that's why it smells.

 Healthy poop sinks slowly.

Your Guided Health Journey

· Health is your True Wealth ·

Our nutrient-depleted soil systems have resulted in mass nutrient deficiencies, even in North America. Consider some basic supplements for your kids and yourself:

MAGNESIUM: 70% of North Americans are deficient in Magnesium, and it's needed in over 300 cellular functions in the body. It is very calming and great to take before bed or put Epsom bath salts in their bath to help them calm down before bed. A deficiency can cause hyperkinetic behavior, anxiety, irritability, and irregular heartbeats.

OMEGA 3S: Over 90% of us are deficient in Omega 3s, which we mainly get through wild fatty fish which many kids don't want to eat. Because we get Omega 6s in our diet very easily and have a harder time getting Omega 3s, we become deficient in Omega 3s relative to our Omega 6s, and therefore, need to supplement. Omega 3s are excellent for the brain, eye, and nervous system health as well as hair, nails, heart, joints, skin, and our immune system. A number of studies have shown that Omega 3s should be recommended first when kids have symptoms of ADHD before using Ritalin, as it's just as effective without the side effects.

VITAMIN D: Over 80% of North Americans are deficient in Vitamin D. It is important for immune health, respiratory health, brain health, our bones and our teeth and it is easy to take with drops under the tongue each day.

VITAMIN C: This is a powerhouse vitamin that is excellent for immune health and so much more. Avoid the orange chewables as they have added sugar! Ascorbic acid is another name for Vitamin C.

And here's a few other facts about minerals for you:

- Potassium deficiency: can show up as allergies / skin issues / constipation / fatigue

- Calcium excess is a good indication of copper toxicity
- Copper in excess: can show up as anxiety, racing mind, it is often present in those diagnosed with ADD / ADHD / Asthma / Allergies, and mood-based disorders, and can often be triggered by a deficiency in zinc and many children are born today with excessive copper levels passed down by mom.
- Low zinc can also cause a weakened gut lining and permeability as well as bed wetting, and a weakened immune system.

A parent can lab test for all of these with just a few strands of hair from your child's head.

To access my "Rainbow Food Chart" to help kids eat a broader variety of foods or book a complimentary consult, click on my Linktree: **https://linktr.ee/yourguidedhealthjourney**

MATTIE MURREY TEGELS

This chapter is dedicated to my father who ignited the fire to pursue greatness and how to find that greatness within myself and others and also to my children, whom I love with all my heart.

THE BUTTERFLY EFFECT:

THE STORY OF A MARINE AND HIS LITTLE BOY WHO DIDN'T TALK

by *Mattie Murrey Tegels*

IF THERE IS ONE THING TO KNOW about me, it is my passion for my field of speech-language pathology. I am one of those lucky people who love what they do. I have worked for over 25 years supporting children and their families with their speech and language challenges as well as those with eating and swallowing difficulties.

When I work with these children, I imagined them as fragile butterflies in the cup of my hands. I breathe life, energy, hope and courage into their wings by improving their communication and eating skills. When they're ready to face the world with their new skills and newfound confidence, I imagine that fragile butterfly flying off onto bigger and better things.

A few years back, one of my clients was a very young nonverbal boy with autism-type tendencies. He was at the point where behaviors were beginning to escalate, and his very loving family had no idea what to do. These behaviors were demonstrated in the only way this boy knew how to express himself, through nonverbal communication. He would throw, scream, pinch, have temper tantrums, and the like—all things that we might see as "bad behavior" but are actually attempts at communication. I worked with him for a short time on his pre-language (gestures, facial expressions, etc.) and language skills, and thought that perhaps an augmentative and alternative communication board (AAC) would help. An AAC system is typically a board or screen with picture symbols that the child presses, and the device says the word to communicate. Research shows that this can be a very effective communication option for non-verbal children so I set up an appointment with our AAC specialist and invited her into one of our sessions.

The boy's mom was not able to make it to the session that day. Instead, he came with his father, a retired Marine with thighs the size of a small girl's waist and arms the size of a small tree trunk. Tattoos covered his biceps and calves. Everything about him resonated strength. This big man walks into my little treatment room with his little boy and fragile hopes. I could see in his eyes that he was feeling loss, grief, and confusion, as well as overarching love.

We got to work. I knew my little friend well and had gotten his favorite toys and put them on the tabletop. Danielle, the AAC specialist, opened her bag and brought out her AAC boards and the fun began. Within minutes, Danielle had taught this little boy how to press buttons to request the toy he wanted. These skills quickly grew to turn-taking, requesting, confirming, and denying. It was absolutely incredible to watch! Who knew he was so capable of learning this new system so quickly? Within 25 minutes, we worked through the basics of screening for the AAC system and selected a device for this youngster. And he himself was requesting, denying and initiating his own wants and needs. Towards the end of the session, the little boy dropped to the floor, put his arms out, and feigned sleep. He suddenly sat up and pressed the button that says, "I'm bored." His father burst into tears of joy because this was his son, his pride and joy. And he was communicating his wants and needs. There was not a single "behavior" the entire session.

This story is why I became a speech-language pathologist—because I believe that our ability to communicate is paramount. It's the thing that makes us human. I am a speech-language pathologist, and I provide skilled evaluations and intervention for speech and language disorders, feeding and swallowing difficulties, voice disorders, and cognitive-linguistic deficits. I also provide parent coaching by supporting parents with children with communication challenges. The basic premise of what I teach is effective communication, both verbal and nonverbal, and I always seek to understand the reasons behind the communication difficulties.

As happy as the father felt in this story, I felt it in a very different way and almost as strong. I had done that. I had helped this boy, and there is nothing more inspiring than that. This is what more parents and caregivers need to feel; it is very empowering.

Whether your child had speech, language, voice, cognitive-communication, social language or eating challenges, to facilitate this transformation, there are three dynamic phases to "You Got This! Speech Therapy and Parent Coaching." They are:

1.UNDERSTANDING

First, seek to understand your child's communication and eating challenges. Does your child have speech difficulties in which they cannot make the sounds accurately and their speech is unintelligible? Maybe your child has language difficulties in which their speech is okay but how they use their words is delayed. These two difficulties can co-exist. Maybe your child is a

"picky eater," and the variety of food they will eat is very limited or they have a verified swallowing disorder, and they are at
risk for choking when they eat and drink. If you suspect autism,
maybe your child has social language challenges, meaning that
they don't connect and communicate with those in their environment. All these primary difficulties may result in second-
ary behavioral challenges such as meltdowns, throwing things,
screaming, crying, and refusing to eat. Ask yourself these four
questions with an open sense of curiosity and openness:

1. How can you better understand your child's communication and eating challenges?

2. What are your child's specific communication and eating
   challenges?

3. What impacts your child's communication and eating success?

4. What are your child's communication and eating strengths,
   and how can you tap into them?

Also, understand the important role that play has for a child.
Did you know it takes approximately 400 repetitions to create
new synapses in the brain unless it's done in play? With play,
it only takes 10 to 20 repetitions. Read that again. Play is IT.
Play is where we make those synaptic connection complete.
Kids don't just play to pass the time. This is their work and their
school. This is where they learn to respond, talk, ask, demand,
and overall, communicate. One you fully understand this, I
can then teach you how you can do the same. The benefits of
this approach are incredible and by understanding that this is
where those neurological connections are made, you will maximize their learning, integration, and success.

You Got This! Speech Therapy and Coaching sees your child's
communication difficulties from their perspective. If we want
to understand our children, we must enter their world, and we

must understand their communication. We need to understand the challenges they face and what's impacting their communication. We must determine what challenges they need to overcome, identify their strengths, and help them tap into their own voice.

2. PREPARING

Second, prepare for the worst and work for the best. When a child has communication and eating difficulties, the fallout can be huge, and with through preparation and engagement with pre-determined strategies, things can improve! Families with these challenges will change their entire plans to avoid private and public meltdowns. A simple trip to the grocery store or an evening out to a restaurant are no longer simple tasks and can turn the best of parents into an embarrassed, angry, bewildered and quivering mess. While parents can't always be prepared for all scenarios, there are ways of identifying patterns of behaviors and proactively implementing strategies to change the scenario from reacting to responding constructively. In preparing for the worst, follow these steps:

1. Think back to your child's specific communication and eating struggles and look for patterns of flare-ups and breakdowns. Also, look for areas of strength and success. Keep track of specific details such as when they occur, who with, preceding events, and contributing factors. Analyze these and develop a customized game plan for overcoming communication breakdowns.

2. Create a dynamic and responsive gameplan for communication and mealtime breakdowns. You plan needs to include a variety of strategies to implement as needed.

3. Implement these strategies in a hierarchical approach. For example, as soon as you notice behaviors emerging, have a

plan to intervene and as the behavior escalates, have additional resources and approaches as needed.

4. Pull in and get buy-in from the stakeholders in your child's world. This is an important element for carrying over of the newly learned skills into a variety of settings. That may include daycare providers, grandparents, or parents of your child's best friend. This is what we call "generalization." We help set up the child for success by giving them the opportunity to practice the new concept being taught in a variety of different settings. By having a consistent approach that's dynamic across a variety of settings, the child learns that what they're learning is relevant in all sorts of scenarios which helps them get their needs met.

5. Research shows us that the number one indicator of how well we do is directly correlated to our ability to reflect on what is happening, self-monitor and correct. Knowing this, continuously reflect on what works well for your child and your family and adjust as needed.

Life can throw any number of curveballs our way. No one expects their child to have a communication challenge such as a speech disorder, a stutter, or a language delay. These challenges don't occur in a vacuum, and they're often accompanied with challenging behaviors. Children didn't ask for these difficulties but it's our job, as adults to be prepared. We need to help our kids navigate life, communication difficulties, and all. Speech-language pathologists are here to help guide.

It's very important to understand that how you respond to your child when those communication difficulties arise lays the groundwork for how successful your child will be. Now, this does not mean that the communication task is on your shoulders alone. But it does mean that as the parent or the caregiver, you are setting the scenario and giving your child the tools to be as successful in their communication as they can be. This means developing a customized game plan for overcoming communication breakdowns.

For example, if your child has a language delay and that means that they're not using their words at each level, then you model for that child how to use those words. If your child has a speech disorder, you can work with your child on modeling the correct speech sounds in ways that are more effective than just "say this sound." You can go above and beyond simply saying "Just tell me what you want." It's really a matter of just setting the stage and the game plan for overcoming those communication breakdowns. And, by seeking first to understand, you understand the perspective of your child. Get curious about why those breakdowns are happening. Ask yourself how you can best support your child in those tough moments (easier said than done). It's so important to also create steps for creating a dynamic and responsive strategy for managing communication breakdowns.

Let's talk about that game plan a little more. Say, for example, your child has an articulation disorder and you and others have difficulty understanding what she is saying. There are certain reactions and behaviors on your part that can make that articulation disorder worse and can initiate a domino effect of other communication and behavior difficulties. For example, the first domino in the chain is your child realizing that other people have trouble understanding them when they talk. The second domino is they can feel shame and begin to avoid talking, and then the third domino is they begin avoiding talking, and the next domino is they begin withdrawing from other kids and isolating themselves to avoid having to talk. This, as you might imagine, limits their social and academic opportunities. But, by shifting the perspective, by understanding the disorder that your child is struggling with, you can support their communication needs. Similarly, if your child has a language delay, you can change that scenario by providing them with successful communication-rich tools that support their communication attempts at the level they are at now.

Let's set the scene a little bit more. Say you are playing at a park and your child has a meltdown. Your role as the caregiver is to support your child in communicating what is wrong. You can ask them open-ended questions such as, "What is wrong?" but that may not be effective as your child may not be able to tell you what is wrong, hence, the meltdown. So, let's take it down a notch and ask your child multiple-choice questions. You can ask, "Are you crying because you are hurt or are you crying because you are sad?" Your child now has some words to use to express themselves. If multiple-choice questions are too hard for your child, shift it down another notch and ask yes and no questions. "Are you hurt?" "Are you mad?" This is the hierarchy of language that you can adjust to meet your child's communication level and help them express their basic wants and needs.

3. CHANGING & ENGAGING

You are not powerless, and your situation is not hopeless. By leading with understanding, empathy, and knowledge, you have the potential and the ability to change and improve your child's communication and eating abilities.

You will be one of the key factors in shaping your child's progress towards improving their overall communication and eating abilities. At You Got This! Speech Therapy and Coaching, we believe that to make these changes, you must start stepping forward, and we believe in walking along side you as you walk alongside your child. In making these first critical steps, there are a few important mindsets to consider:

1. You are walking alongside your child and learning alongside with them what works and what doesn't work. You are

partners. You will still maintain your parental authority, but you will be at their level of investment in the process.

2. You will learn to see things from your child's perspective. Since this is the view with which they see the world, you will need to understand and see the world through their view and adopt their experiences.

3. Be comfortable stepping away from black and white, right and wrong and change the focus to learning and implementing. This is magical when is occurs, and when this "crossover" occurs, the momentum in success accelerates.

4. "I never lose. Either I win or I learn," said Nelson Mandela. Loving your child, working with your child, and helping them learn, grow, and succeed is never about losing or winning or being right and wrong. It is about growing, learning, and doing your best and it is about supporting your child in being their best.

5. By understanding the hierarchy of modeling for your child, you can better support them. Therapy and coaching is an approach for walking alongside your child in their communication challenges. "A teacher takes a hand, opens the mind, and touches a heart." As the parent, you can be the teacher. I as the speech-language pathologist can be the teacher. And as a parent coach, I will be your teacher and guide. As I take your hand, open your mind, and touch your heart. In turn, you take your child's hand, open their minds and touch your child's heart. Being able to see things from your child's perspective is an incredibly important piece in changing that conversation.

Recently, my 24-year-old son sold a house making a profit of roughly $140,000. So, as any good parent does, I took him to a financial planner who was going to help him safely tuck away this money. As my son sat across from the planner, I could see his hands trembling, as he held the unopened envelope that contained a $140,000 check. It was more money than he had ever held before. I told him that he could keep the check and it would remain $140,000 or, he could invest it and watch it grow. I asked the financial planner to average 7% interest across 40 years, which is when my son would turn 64, his retirement age. His $140,000 check will have grown into $2.3 million because that initial investment was done at the right time. While that takes patience, the payoff is huge.

Similarly, and even more so, when we invest in our children, the payoffs are astronomical. Research shows that children who are delayed in speech and language skills are also delayed in many other areas of their life. That's why speech and language therapy and parent coaching is so profound. It has the potential to affect all areas of the child's life. When that happens, there is no better job in the world than the one I have the privilege of doing.

When I was young, I always wanted to wear glasses because my dad wore glasses. I thought it was so funny to put his glasses on and trot around the room. And I was always so amazed at how blurry things were. But for my father, those glasses were the perfect prescription for his eyes. For me, they didn't work. So, if I asked my father to read something, he needed his prescription glasses. And when our children need to communicate, they need to communicate through their lenses, their mouth, their mind, and we need to support that. You Got This Speech Therapy focuses on learning and implementing the skills that a child needs to be successful in their communication attempts. Either we win or we learn, but we never lose. You Got This Speech Therapy and Coaching supports you and your child in overcoming those communication barriers.

So, if you are like my Marine parent, if you love a child with communication challenges, or feeding and eating challenges, take that opportunity to understand that your child is different and has unique needs and challenges. And that's all. It doesn't make them wrong. It doesn't make them weak. It doesn't make them bad. A good child is not defined by their behavior or their communication challenges. Your child is defined by who they are as tiny little human beings. And it is our challenge as parents, caregivers, coaches, and speech-language pathologists to hold these children gently in the cup of our hands until they are strong enough to fly on their own. You got this!

Find Me

WEBSITE: **www.yougothisspeechtherapy.com**

EMAIL: **mattie@freshslp.com**

PODCAST: The Missing Link for SLPs

JOANNE LIGHT

*I am dedicating this chapter to one of my mentors,
Dr Ali Lankerani, who pushed me out of my comfort
zone. But the support I have had in dipping my
educational leadership and consulting toes into
entrepreneurial endeavors has been mostly provided
by my husband, Jonathan Light.*

CONSEQUENCES OF PARENTING FROM FEAR: LET'S CHANGE IT UP!

by *Joanne Light*

PARENTING IS AN EXHILARATING and exhausting job and likely the hardest one you will ever have. Even folks who have no children are likely to agree with that statement.

We teach our children so many things and, unfortunately, one is fear. It is intended as a means of protection. But too often, we let that fear be a baseline home for our kids and *for* us.

Fear can be crippling. From the moment we first hold our newborn, fear grips our motherly hearts and argues regularly against letting go. After all, the world seems like a frightening and dangerous place. The list of things that terrify us is endless – disabilities, pandemic, school shootings, sleeplessness, bullying, internet predators, mean friends, loneliness, drugs, failure, etc. Need I say more? I totally agree and understand. If, for example, I were to ask you "Have you been afraid something bad will happen to your child? Or "Have you thought you might mess them up for life? "Or "Have you worried you can't protect them all the time?"

I believe every parent would affirm that last question, and what is so troubling about that one is that it is true—you can't. Intellectually, most parents know they cannot protect their children from anything bad happening, but if that is your go-to thought, you are likely parenting from a place of fear. This creates ongoing and heart-crushing anxiety and prevents you from seeing the good that is happening, from being grateful and from enjoying your child.

Now, I am not saying that it is intentional to be anxious and fearful, nor am I saying that you even realize it. Let's take a look at where this fear comes from and how it is manifested.

There are plenty of good reasons to be fearful. Society has imposed, particularly in western culture, unrealistic expectations, stereotypical versions of success and the value of winning.

If you look inward and contemplate how you were parented, fear, punishment and yelling may sound all too familiar. Just trying to modify that approach or change the mistakes we believe our parents made naturally affects our parenting styles. That evokes fear. On the other hand, if you want to reproduce your parents' mode and you feel incapable whether because of economics, social situations, or your emotional state, that too evokes fear.

If you are waking up at night ruminating "What ifs?" like "What if he doesn't make the team?" What if she has no friends?" What if they are doing drugs?" What if they hate me?' "What if they are gender challenged?" You are then both a sleep deprived and an anxious parent.

Anxiety is about the past or the future and rarely not about what is going on right now. We parents also catastrophize: "Well, I think my daughter is getting fat … she is fat. My sister was fat and she never had a meaningful relationship in her entire life." Or "My teen is lying to me all the time and I know it. My brother was a liar, and he never held down a job." Your brain just doesn't stop. This is also evidence you may be parenting from a place of fear.

So ... Maybe you are thinking, is that really such a bad thing? We all want the best for our children, and their health and safety are paramount. If threatened by real or imagined events, our blood pressure skyrockets. It doesn't matter if the tiger isn't chasing you, it is an instinctive reaction. We must contemplate what the result of that reaction may be. Do we lecture, freak out and try to fix? Yes, we all do sometimes. However, we absolutely must consider each situation on its merits and be mindful of our fear and anxiety.

Ask yourself questions: "What is making me so afraid at this time? Am I tired? Am I just frustrated from work? Am I angry at my spouse? What is really going on?" Is my fear, flight & freeze brain making good choices? Be curious. If you think your child is depressed, is there evidence of that? If you worry your child is being left out, what has happened to make you think so? Try to determine what is triggering your fear. What is the scenario for your trigger—homework, morning routine, late curfew, slamming doors? Use the pause technique. Stop and breathe deeply. Be sure you have made reasonable and consistent rules and avoid the circumstances that can trigger you. Working on how to avoid those situations is freeing and helps to reduce anxiety and fear.

The danger in parenting from a place of fear is your tendency to fix every problem. You rush to school if they left homework on the kitchen table. You bring them their forgotten lunch and notebooks. You call the teacher for every complaint your child has of mistreatment. You edit their papers and put the finishing touches on their diorama or science project. All these efforts are to protect our children and to make certain they are seen as competent. But we do a huge disservice because without natural consequences, our child will not learn to remember things or take responsibility for themselves. They may even come to assume you believe they are incompetent and unable to defend themselves or complete tasks without you. Your worry provides some control and fixes for the moment, but it isn't healthy for your child or for you. We do it because we worry about others' judgments. We fret that we aren't good enough, our kids are not good enough, or our friends and family won't see our kids as good enough. Fear of being judged is a great contributor to parents' fear.

We have established that we live in an age of anxiety and of pervasive social media. We often believe our children, particularly our tweens and teens, are in constant danger. We then get on the crazy train of overscheduling, overdoing and overreacting.

We helicopter or snowplow. Those are terms for styles of parenting that are frequently written about today. The hovering, helicoptering parent who fixes everything described above, or perhaps worse, the snowplowing parent who eliminates every possible obstacle for their child so they can be successful and never experience disappointment or failure. That approach is so exhausting. In addition, the parent is not modeling self-care at all and can become burned out or even resentful.

Anxiety is contagious; the neurons spread like a virus. Your anxiety becomes your child's go-to mode of feeling and reacting. Kids who are protected from failure have a harder time learning the value of making mistakes and the value of problem solving. Feelings of self-doubt and irresponsibility up the ante for shame and depression. When you wonder why you suggested you might be able to help them raise their B in math to an A, they worry about your disappointment and anger. They shut down. When communicating with your kids, ask yourself if you are meeting their needs or yours.

Okay. Let's take a break. Honestly, I am not trying to make you feel you are 'messing up' or make you worry about 'messing up.' I am driving home the point that fear is the villain. It is the monster hiding under the bed. Remember growing up, you worried about monsters under the bed and your parents tried to dissuade you – perhaps sweetly but dismissively – "There is no such thing as monster." But you know better, so fear and anxiety overtake us. I totally get it. I have been there.

My oldest daughter suffers with anxiety, paralyzing anxiety. It began when she entered high school. She lost interest in playing the piano, doing her schoolwork, and being with her best friends. With a new crowd, she abused drugs and was clearly struggling. I responded with fear, anxiety, and many "what if" worries about her future. My anxiety increased hers, contributing toher avoidance of me. It also affected the entire family; she had two younger siblings. Everyone who loved and cared for me worried as well. It took a long time to get the right help and to change the relationship and reach connection.

Fear is bad because it robs you of the present. Too much focus is on what you worry about and what you don't want to happen. Fear is mostly bad because it hides your best self. Dr. Shefali Tsabary, a clinical psychologist and conscious family therapist suggests, "When your relationship is as rooted in fear as it is in love; when the ratio of fear to love is skewed so that fear wins, our approach to our children creates the opposite of what we hope for."

I am proposing that you parent from a place of trust. That is my message today. If you parent from a place of trust, it changes the milieu from anxiety to calm. A trusting parent knows their child has watched them model calm and problem-solving behavior. Then, they feel confident that their child can figure out the issues arising in school and social situations. Furthermore, that parent knows their child will ask for help when they need it. Fear breeds controlling, self-serving parenting and interferes with caring and trust. Parents who respond to their children from a place of trust have kids who trust themselves and become the adults they are meant to be.

You can endlessly read about parenting styles: conscious parenting, joyful parenting, peaceful parenting, and positive parenting. Tips, strategies and nuance may differ, but all will advise you that the critical ingredient to parenting from a place of trust is connection. The bond you create with your child in the earliest days and through their tween and teen years will assure greater chances for their emotional well-being through their adult lives.

I encourage parents to adopt the emotional intelligence skill base as one means of connecting, restoring and repairing connection when necessary. Self-awareness and regulation of your own emotions are key. If you have been exposed to the teachings of emotional Intelligence, you leverage your self-awareness to build that and create resilience in your child.

What we do in the heat of the moment makes all the difference. Respond to those tantrums, meltdowns and disappointments with empathy and true listening. Our children feel understood and not judged. They begin to understand that you are connecting, not correcting. Once you recognize you are parenting from a place of trust and love, you will not step back into fear.

When we develop and celebrate our self-awareness, we can let go of generational biases which may be our history but don't have to be our destiny. Dan Siegel, psychiatrist, professor, and author says, "The best indicator of a child's well-being is the parent's self-understanding." "Mindset: The New Science of Personal Transformation."

> "The best indicator of a child's well-being is the
> parent's self-understanding."
> —DAN SIEGEL

Because you connect and encourage communication through listening without judgment, without interruption, without a fix and without ego, you are modeling trust. They are watching you all the time – Yes, even (and especially) your tweens and teens. Your empathy enhances connection by letting them process the situation and make healthy choices and mistakes. When you lose it, and we all do, restore the connection through apology and telling them how much you love them. William Martin, an American author, and philosopher of Taoism reminds us, "You do not have to make your children into wonderful people. You only have to remind them they are wonderful."

> "You do not have to make your children into
> wonderful people. You only have to remind them
> they are wonderful."
> —WILLIAM MARTIN

So, dismiss the monster under your bed. No longer accept anxiety as the ruler of your thoughts and actions. It isn't about perfection. It is about practicing the skills of communication, of expressing emotions and of listening. You can then work on creating the environment where your children can become who they are meant to be and to trust that they will get there. You have given them the gifts of space and endless support. They know you have their back. Trust trumps fear—both theirs and yours.

Notes from the Author:

Readers,

I would love to have your feedback. You can reach me directly by email **Joanne@joannehlight.com** or by scheduling a chat **https://joannehlightcoaching.as.me/**

You can learn more about me and my philosophy on my website at **https://www.Joannehlight.com**

Also, you may want to visit my LinkedIn account where I post thoughts – my own and those of many other experts. **https://www.linkedin.com/in/joanne_empathy_light**

My free gift to you about parent burnout is available at **https://joannehlight.com/overcome-burnout-now/** as is my recent contribution of six videos on the Amazing Parent Network: **https://rolemodelmaker.thrivecart.com/apn-fes-joanne/**

Parenting is enchanting and challenging, so do not be hesitant to seek help. I have heard clients say, "I used to be a nice person before I had children" (LOL). I love listening to parents so they understand a.) they are not alone b.) they need to get that so much begins with them.

I am grateful to Jaci and Lil for encouraging me to contribute a chapter and to be a part of a wonderful network of professionals and experts. Writing has always been a love and a part of my endeavors.

Joanne H Light EdD.; CLC
Parent Empowerment Coach
PHONE: 781-883-8544
https://linktr.ee/joannehlight

Your Story Your Journey Your Change

JEANNIE BALDOMERO

This chapter is dedicated to my mother, Teresita dela Rosa, for braving the storm of my teenage years with no support and to my teenage daughter, Ava Liana, who makes my job as her mama easy.

MOM, REMOVE THAT GUILT AND GET REAL WITH YOUR RELATIONSHIP WITH YOUR TEEN DAUGHTER

by *Jeannie Baldomero*

I'M AN AVID READER, health fanatic, wife and mom of three. I grew up a Catholic school girl who's first boyfriend was a gang member, and now I live in the suburbs of San Diego with my handsome husband (who is not the said gang member) and three amazing children: two teenagers and one young adult. I have also mentored tween and teen girls through growth groups in my local community church.

I must say that parenting has been a roller coaster ride of twists and turns and unpredictable dips that can throw us off our feet.

I wouldn't trade it for the world. I have many passions, coffee being a high priority. I love unleashing my inner creativity through various creative outlets. As a former educator and as a homeschooling family for several years, my passion for healthy families and zeal to impact young teen girls has led me to partner with moms to guide them in creating healthy relationships with their teens.

I am passionate about serving people to be their best and helping young teen girls thrive in their true identity.

When I reflect on my life's experiences and the path that has brought me to who I am today, the pivotal and significant time in my life was when I was 13 years old. It was a time where my childhood and the trajectory of my adulthood collided. It was a crucial time in my life. Thankfully, now as an adult, entrepreneur, and mom, I have reflected on my past to make decisions with my current circumstance and relationships to use them as a platform to help others.

Why 13? It was the year my mom said, "I don't know who you are anymore." It was the year I made many dumb mistakes, which then led to a cascade of other mistakes in my adult life. I was that young girl that needed guidance, that needed help even when I rejected it. I needed a mentor to guide me, not my inexperienced friends to lead me.

This is why my heart is here with young teen girls. I am here to help girls lessen the voices of the lies they hear about themselves and amplify the truth about them.

I think back to how my mom tried her best with what she knew and what she was capable of. I wrote "ROOTED" for her and moms like her that desperately want to understand their changing girl and how they can help build a unique relationship with her.

In short, I equip moms of teenage girls to parent confidently without risking their relationship.

STEP 1: SEEK FIRST TO UNDERSTAND

Moms are notorious for imposing self-guilt. It's normal to feel like you are failing when it comes to parenting your tween/teenage daughter. However, we can allow that failure to affect the way we relate to our daughters. It's vital to discover your ideal relationship with your daughter, the reality of your current relationship, take responsibility for your part of the relationship and the changes occurring in your daughter as an adolescent.

YOUR IDEAL RELATIONSHIP WITH YOUR DAUGHTER:

Moms need to dream about their ideal relationship with their daughters.

If I had a magic wand and I waved it over you, what would your ideal relationship with your teen daughter look like? It will not be perfect, but being clear with what you desire will help you understand how to pick and choose your battles.

It is human nature to look sideways at other moms and their relationships with their daughters. We convince ourselves that this is how a relationship should look like. Comparison robs us of the richness in relationships with the people close to us.

As each child is unique, so is each relationship. You know what you desire out of your relationship with your daughter.

> **TRY THIS**: Brainstorm a list full of keywords that describe your ideal relationship with your teenage daughter.

THE REALITY OF YOUR CURRENT RELATIONSHIP:

Moms need to understand the reality of where their current relationship is with their daughter.

When we understand where we are at, we can be honest with ourselves about the work and change that needs to happen in the relationship.

I sat one day listening to a sermon on parenting. A light bulb clicked as I began listening more intently. The key to parenting in the teen stage is our role as parents.

Most moms are stuck in a role their daughter has already out-grown or is shoved prematurely into a friend relationship. We're not taught how to transition between the seasons of parenting.

Here's a simple way to understand parenting in 4 seasons (Thanks to my friend Mike Meeks, Pastor Emeritus at Eastlake Church, for breaking it down):

1. **Nursing - parenting a child from ages 0-3**

    - Providing for basic needs: feeding, bathing, changing.
    - Child is 100% dependent on their parents.

2. **Queen/King - parenting from 3-10**

    - Children are more independent.
    - Rules and boundaries are needed.
    - Parents are the rulers of the house.
    - What parents say goes.

3. **Coach - parenting from 10-18**

    - Adolescent stage.

- Kids change physically, mentally, emotionally.
- Parents are guides.
- Parents are more on the sidelines than calling the plays.
- Kids are the players who get to choose.
- Wider boundaries are set.

4. **Friend - parenting 18+**

- Children are adults.
- Parents establish a friendship.
- Parents are counselors and a source of wisdom.

These ages are estimated depending on the maturity of each child. Relationships between teen daughters and mothers are commonly tested likely because our roles are displaced.

Stages of Parenting

This chart illustrates our parental authority vs friendship. You'll see that authority is high during the Queen/King season and decreases in the Friend season. As opposed to friendship, it is low during the Queen/King season and increases as we approach the Friend season. What's interesting is the visual crossroads of authority and friendship intersect during the Coach season, which explains why parenting during the adolescent years is a difficult one to navigate through.

It's important to understand where you see your role right now. Maybe you find yourself hanging out in the Queen stage longer than you should or rushing your relationship into the Friend stage quicker than your relationship needs. Understanding this will help bring clarity to your current relationship with your daughter.

TAKING RESPONSIBILITY FOR YOUR PART OF THE RELATIONSHIP

Moms need to uncover their own expectations and actions that may contribute to their current relationship with their teenage daughter.

As moms, we need to establish authority from the very day our children are born. How we establish boundaries, rules and communication can be based on some factors.

1. How we were raised

2. On our insecurities

3. What we've learned

Rules are meant to keep an individual safe from others and themselves. They are non-negotiable, unbendable and require a consequence if broken.

Boundaries, on the other hand, are the gray areas. They are flexible, negotiable, and allow for choices. However, when crossed, consequences will occur.

Communication is how we relate to others. Tone, word choice and timing all factor into communication. Communication can either hurt or deepen relationships.

We can reflect on these three factors and how they currently affect our relationship with our daughters. Most times, you'll find they fall under Queen stage with little room for independence your tween/teen girl so desperately wants.

A coach's top three roles:

1. Models choices

2. Sets realistic boundaries & consequences

3. An empathetic guide who imparts wisdom where the choice is up to the person.

> **TRY THIS**: Observe for a day or even a week, your responses, expectations, actions, and conversations with your daughter. What stage do they tend to fall under? Look at your current rules and boundaries your daughter is allowed or not allowed to do. What stage of parenting do they fall under?

THE CHANGES OCCURRING IN YOUR DAUGHTER

Moms need to understand the changes happening to their daughter in the adolescent stage in order to connect better with her.

John Hopkins Medicine and Stanford's Children Health agree puberty-related changes in girls happen before boys between the ages of 8-13.

It's important we understand what girls go through:

1. They do not understand what is happening to them.

- They tend to feel insecure, scared, and have self-doubt

2. They gain:

- Abstract thinking
- Concerns for social issues, politics, and philosophy
- Ability to set goals
- Awareness of others and comparing oneself.

3. They begin to desire independence and control

- Wants independence from parents
- Seeks a partner to coexist with
- Peer influence and acceptance become very important
- Romantic and sexual relationships become important
- May be in love
- Capable of long-term commitment in relationships

When we understand the biological and social-emotional changes that are happening in our daughters, we can understand the importance of our role as a coach in this stage of their development. We are able to reestablish clear expectations and understand the behaviors our daughter reflects according to her changes and how we can adjust accordingly with honesty, empathy and authentic conversations.

STEP 2: PREPARE FOR THE WORST

The adolescent stage is a roller coaster of emotions for both you and your teen. The drama your once sweet girl is suddenly creating in your home, often give you no clue how to approach these situations. There is freedom in clarifying core values and reestablishing boundaries.

CLARIFYING CORE VALUES

Moms need to gain clarity and understand the core values of their family and that of their teen's.

Values are an unwavering guide to navigating life's journey. Core values are the fundamental beliefs of a person. These guiding principles dictate behavior and can help people understand the difference between right and wrong.

Getting clear on what your family values are will help your daughter understand what should be valued most. Her behavior and actions will be measured against them. This takes responsibility off your chest. You are establishing that you are not the bad guy. These values will challenge her choices and actions accordingly.

Clarifying your core values can bring your relationship to a deeper level. When you understand what your daughter values most, you can respect her choices, challenge her on the ones you may disagree with and communicate how these may look like in her life.

Core values are the foundation of your "playbook" as you coach your daughter through navigating life. You are creating opportunities to refine her, and open doors for authentic conversations.

> **TRY THIS**: Stop taking responsibility for your teenager's choices and hold them accountable to your family's core values. I have a free guide on Clarifying Core Values that directs you and your family towards discovering what you value most. You can access it through the link provided at the end of this chapter.

REESTABLISHING BOUNDARIES

Moms need to establish clear expectations in order to focus on what matters most, a healthy genuine relationship with their daughter.

Boundaries are the guardrails to life. Boundaries and accountability help shape your teen towards living out her values.

Your teen daughter desires control over her life. This is where we shift our parenting perspective as her coach.

When we look at the boundaries that are currently in place, we can reassess them based on the following. Do they:

1. Foster independence (age appropriate)
2. Set clear boundaries
3. Create rules that uphold what YOU believe in.
4. Allow freedom for her to choose within the boundaries
5. Follow up with a consequence, natural or agreed upon

Boundaries will be pushed, they will be tested, and they will be challenged. I love this quote from Mark Gregston, author of *Tough Guys and Drama Queens*, "The mark of a good parent is not necessarily a well-behaved child."

"The mark of a good parent is not necessarily a well-behaved child."
—MARK GREGSTON

The coaching season is one of the most difficult stages moms will go through. But, with proper communication skills, you will work through this turbulent stage while growing your relationship with her.

> **TRY THIS**: Look at your house rules and boundaries. Do they need to be updated so you can coach through them with your daughter?

STEP 3: CHANGE THE CONVERSATION

Communication is vital in the teen stage, yet pretty confusing as to when, how, and what to say. Your daughter craves to be loved and to belong. The way we communicate with her makes all the difference in creating an authentic relationship together. Communication requires creating a safe space.

CREATING A SAFE SPACE

Moms need to understand that communication during the coaching season will dictate how much their daughters will receive guidance, open up in conversation, and trust them as parents.

Mark Gregston also gave some great points on authority, "Authority alone is not your friend. Authority needs to be cushioned with relationships. It builds trust." Your daughter will change because of relationships, not authority.

"Authority alone is not your friend. Authority needs to be cushioned with relationships. It builds trust."
—MARK GREGSTON

Communication is the foundation of a relationship with your daughter.

Establishing a safe space for open conversations requires a few things to consider:

1. **TIMING IS EVERYTHING** - bad timing equates to judgment. No matter how gentle you come across, if the timing is not ideal, you will come across as judgmental, and the walls will come up.

2. **KEEP THE LISTENING EARS ON.** What matters most to your daughter is that she is heard and that you understand what she is saying. Acknowledge her. She will likely continue to share with you and involve you in the conversation.

3. **CHANGE YOUR PARENTING STYLE AND EMBRACE YOUR COACH ROLE.** You remember what it was like being a teen. You understand the changes she is going through. When she feels understood by you, she will be more willing to be open to your guidance since she knows you have her best interests at heart.

The teen years may feel like they last forever, but in reality, it all moves at a blink of an eye. Your daughter needs to feel loved and feel belonging. So, drop the guilt. Dig deep to understand your current relationship and the changes she's going through. Your ideal relationship with her can be created with a simple shift in your role. Reestablishing some clear boundaries and an understanding of communication will free you to cultivate an authentic and genuine relationship with your daughter.

I have some amazing resources to help you connect with your teen that you can use right now in our free Resource Library, which include positive affirmations and my personal favorite, Clarifying Core Values Guide.

I believe every mom needs a community of women who get it. Quoting the familiar phrase, "It takes a village," it does indeed take one to raise a girl through this season. Let's connect. I would love to hear your story. You can reach me at **hello@jeanniebaldomero.com** or visit me at **www.jeanniebaldomero.com** for free access to the Resource Library and more information on the ROOTED program supporting healthy mother-daughter relationships.

JACKIE BAILEY

I dedicate this chapter to:

-my grandchildren Samuel, Miles, Etta, and Cece. If I'd taken my life all those years ago, I would never have known the joy of being your grandmother.

-children, teens and adults around the world who survive the effects of trauma every day. You'll be stronger than you can imagine once you conquer this, and you will conquer.

- all those who don't believe you're worthy of being heard. Your voice is your gift to the world. Speak out. I hear you.

HOW TO SAVE YOUR SILENCED CHILD

by *Jackie Bailey*

I HAVE DEDICATED my life to healing from childhood trauma, forgiving those responsible, and paying it forward as much as possible.

DON'T TELL ANYONE

I would be awakened in the middle of the night hearing his ankles crack outside my bedroom door.

"Please, God, don't let it happen again."

I tucked my blankets tighter around me. I would not make it easy for him.

When it was over, he would always warn, "Don't tell anyone."

I did not. I was cautious to initiate conversations, afraid I might "tell" something I should not. The command not to tell kept me from being who I was meant to be. It is awful being silenced and swindled out of childhood.

The abuse continued through my teenage years. Most of my life was miserable yet managed. Until one day another child's innocence was on the line and under my abuser's constant control.

By then, I was a married woman with young children. In crisis, I had three choices: (1) shamefully reveal my secret while risking the so-called stability of my family; (2) shamefully stay silent while risking the life and happiness of an innocent child whom I could save; (3) shamefully choose suicide and remain silenced forever.

I alone knew of the threat. Who would protect my children if I died? It was up to me to break years of silence no matter the risk. I would stay alive because I loved my children more than I hated myself.

I'VE A SECRET

Those are the three words I declared to my husband. He was relieved because he finally understood why I was miserable. Next, I broke my silence to those whom I felt would advocate for me. I was believed by most. My admission forced awareness about the abuser and saved the life of the intended child ... and my own children.

My healing journey lasted years, and through it all I recognized increasingly the power of my voice. Freedom from silence was strangely sensational. I was finally being heard, and my words were being shared with fellow survivors.

I was well on my way to uttering three marvelously magical words which I never thought possible.

I FORGIVE YOU

My counselor told me early on, "...if you are not working toward forgiveness, you will never heal from the trauma you've suffered." I chuckled at the suggestion of forgiving then. It seemed as impossible as picking up a semi-truck and throwing it across the road.

Years passed before I realized I indeed had reached this pinnacle of healing. The last step was to tell my former abuser, and I traveled over 1,000 miles (more than 1780 km) for that purpose. Through some weird twist of fate, I had been holding the key to his prison cell. By stating, "I forgive you" the sufferer had become savior and the criminal had become a casualty. Healing was completed for me, and healing had commenced for him. Forgiveness freed both the abused and the abuser.

DON'T TELL ANYONE. Words which altered the life of an innocent child.

I'VE A SECRET. Words which converted pain into potential.

I FORGIVE YOU. Words which restored love, reversed wrong, and returned power to two unlikely beings.

Three different words spoken at three contrasting times through the phases of my life's journey. To some, the words are insignificant, yet as a part of life's sketch, they are a symbolic depiction of the power of voice.

Words were my superpower. Words can be your superpower too. It is my life's purpose to help children and teens don their superhero capes and recognize the dynamic influence their voices have on everyone who hears them.

Three words now represent what the curriculum *The Speak Feed Lead Project* offers to youth and adults, and describe the outcome of the organizational mission:

SPEAK | FEED | LEAD

The Speak Feed Lead Project prepares adults and children to shine sharing their heartfelt messages, and to *Speak* with power, *Feed* others in word and deed, and *Lead* with positive influence. As I parent and grandparent, I have unknowingly silenced my loved ones. If you are like me, you have made similar statements to these:

"Because I said so..."

"Just be quiet."

"If you can't say anything nice, don't say anything at all."

"You don't need to understand why, you just need to obey me."

"You're such a tattletale."

Have you ever considered the ways your words silence your child(ren) and rip the cape from their super shoulders? If children understand through your words that their self-expression is unwelcome or unimportant, they believe you.

Once children enter school, they are graded on how they express what someone of authority deems is necessary and important. They are graded on spelling instead of feeling. They show and tell, rather than share and tell. Values of empathy, self-expression, and self-love are replaced by an indoctrination of self-loathing, self-confusion, and activism.

When the awkwardness of puberty commences, our 'tweens and teens may lose their sense of belonging and have no one in whom they can confide.

SOCIAL MEDIA HAS BECOME THE SOURCE OF OUR TEENS' SELF-ESTEEM

Predators and pariahs are actively engaging with our wounded, silenced youth; encouraging lies or exaggerations to be liked and acknowledged. To elevate themselves, kids learn they must knock others down. Some youth act on ridiculously risky behaviors just to get attention.

Stories of cyber-bullying, cyber-sexual abuse, and cyber-blackmail are prolific in a 24/7 cycle of which there is no escape. Without self-worth and watchful parents, our children are easy prey. Human trafficking is a booming industry. Unintentionally, parents, teachers, and even religious leaders are desensitizing youth who may find it alluring and unable to free themselves from the web.

BREATHE

I have taken you on a journey to some deep, dark places, so take a deep, distracting, discerning breath. Change is coming. I am going to teach you to open the door to the world of your child. I will show you ways to discover where they are and invite them back to a world of safety, self-expression, and self-love. You must be willing to sacrifice your all-knowing, I'm-right-and-you're-wrong attitude to make this happen and save your family.

Stand at the threshold with me, take my hand, and let us begin.

STEP ONE: STOP TALKING AT YOUR CHILDREN

Make note of how many people a day talk to your kids. You, other parents, siblings, teachers, friends, coaches, bullies, employers, authority figures, strangers, extended family, etc. Consider how many statements are coming at them from people whom they are reacting to, and not initiating real engagement with.

- "You're going to be late."
- "Don't forget your lunch."
- "Sit down. Class is starting."
- "Answer these questions."
- "Read this chapter."
- "Give a report."
- "Stand up."
- "Sit down."
- "Run a lap."
- "Put the dishes away."

Of all the statements being deposited into your child's brain account on a daily basis, how many are assets versus liabilities of self-value? Words are a superpower, and they can also be poisonous.

STEP 2: ASK MORE QUESTIONS

To make gains in a child's self-esteem, stop talking and start asking questions. Take a cue from child development. All parents at one time are exhausted by the unending questions of a young child. Most parents would gladly remove *why?* from their child's vocabulary.

If curiosity and questioning are such large components of early childhood development, we should consider the importance of curiosity and questioning in our parental and family development.

I was age 10 when my parents learned a friend of theirs had been arrested for molesting his daughters. While reading the article revealing this man's crimes, my mother commented to me, "I'm so glad he never did that to you."

How could I shatter my mother's gladness by revealing he HAD done that to me?

By making a statement rather than asking a question, my mother shut down any chance I would tell her then, or ever, about her friend, Ray, and his horrible acts on me.

Once when I was 15, my mother came into my room and sat on the edge of my bed. She must have suspected something was causing my unhappiness, since her attempt at heart-to-heart talks were rare.

"Are you letting someone do something to you they shouldn't?"

My mother's horrific choice of words in her question kept me silent about abuse happening to me right under her nose. She led me to believe I was at fault. I was "letting" it happen. I cannot express the damage done that night by the poisonous words of my mother.

TRY ASKING THESE TYPES OF QUESTIONS INSTEAD

- "What was the best part of your day?"
- "How does it make you feel when someone says that to you?"
- "What skill are you most happy you can do?"
- "What's the secret of your success?"
- "Will you teach me how to do that?"
- "What do you feel you should do now?"
- "What are you feeling right now?"
- "Have you felt this way before?"

With this type of language, the door is wide open, and in the process, you will have discovered your child's hiding place.

STEP 3: LISTEN, THEN RESPOND WITHOUT JUDGMENT

Nature tells us that we should listen twice as much as we talk, which is why we have two ears and only one mouth. If we ever discovered the owner's manual for our ears, we would learn those two organs were designed not to work when our gums are flapping, and that our eyes should always be open and fully engaged with the person we are talking to.

If you feel your children do not listen to you, I guarantee they learned by your example. Put down the damn device in your hand when your kids are talking to you. It may be an emergency, so STOP, LOOK, and LISTEN as all the safety prevention manuals say.

Instagram-surfing/hologram-parenting will be conclusive evidence to your kids it is a waste of breath to answer your questions because you are not listening anyway. That is why you get "fine," "good," or simply a grunt as an answer to most questions. You have trained them well.

When you do get an answer from your child and you react with, "What?! I told you to be careful with that!" or "I am so disappointed in you" or "How could you have embarrassed me like that?" all you have done is reinforced the idea that sharing information with you causes mama drama.

LADIES AND GENTLEMEN, CONVERSATION IS NOW CLOSED

I know how difficult it is to be a parent. It is challenging to be young, too. Confidence in communication, conversation, and listening must be used effectively if we are to keep values of empathy, self-expression, and self-love intact.

Sharing my story of healing by using my voice is the foundation for *The Speak Feed Lead Project*. I passionately believe we can heal from all trauma by using our superpower of words to speak our truth, share our stories, and understand that we are worthy to be heard.

Programs provided by *The Speak Feed Lead Project* are ongoing to support kids grades 4-5, grades 6-8, high school through college, and adults. Every phase of life you and your offspring are in will be enhanced when your voice is spring-loaded and ready when needed with the proper language. Effective speakers are effective leaders, however, leaders are not naturally effective speakers. It takes training and coaching from an expert.

After using my voice to heal, I used my message to compete. I was a semi-finalist in The World Championships of Public Speaking, placing in the top 98 of 33,000 competitors. I could never have imagined impacting the lives of hundreds of people as I have by telling what I was told for so many years not to speak about.

I ENCOURAGE YOU TO CONSIDER THREE MORE WORDS: SHARE YOUR STORY

You and your children need to be heard. You are worthy of being heard. Do not be silenced any longer or kept from inspiring change in others. Enhance the dynamic of your family by enrolling your children in our public speaking programs. As a nonprofit, there are fees to accommodate any budget.

When a child is confident enough to speak out, they will not be as impacted by trauma as will a child who is not confident to speak. You will save your silenced child.

HEATHER GRECO

This chapter is dedicated to my cookie monsters:
Theodore, Eliana, and Zachary.

CHAOS CONTROL SYSTEM: 3 TIME-SAVING TIPS FOR EVERY PARENT

by *Heather Greco*

IT'S NOT BREAKING NEWS that moms work long hours and feel that the week is a never-ending series of tasks to complete. A study conducted by Welch's found that working moms clock an average of 98 hours each week, equivalent to working 2.5 full-time jobs. A study of 2,000 American mothers with kids between five and 12 years old found that the average mother "clocks in" at 6:23 a.m. and "clocks out" at 8:31 p.m., for an average workday of 14 hours.

Hi! I'm Heather Greco, an efficiency expert and chaos coordinator. Following the crumbs in the chaos is a full-time job as a busy, single mom of three young children. I am the CEO and founder of Chaos n' Cookies and the host of the Chaos n' Cookies Podcast. *Podcast Magazine* named me a top 40 under 40 podcast host and ranked the podcast #26 in the top 50 Moms in Podcasts. Keeping moms from crumbling is my main objective by sharing possible and sustainable ways to control the chaos at home and free up moms' schedule.

I teach sustainable, time-saving tips and tricks that will work with any busy schedule. This is more than just your average time-blocking strategy and color-coded calendar. I'm talking systems that are "set it and forget it!"

When going through my divorce, I not only had to continue my mommy tasks, but I also had to take on my ex-husband's duties and responsibilities. In addition to these tasks on my plate, I also needed to go back to the workforce and get a full-time job while trying to sustain the business that I worked so hard to build. When I was married, I barely had time to handle my part and now I had to do it all. I remember asking myself, "How am I going to survive? How am I going to do this all by myself?"

No matter how defeated I felt at that moment, my situation was still the same, and I needed to get creative, fast. The main problem I wanted to solve was how I could make it easier for my children to do more at home with less of my help. Every home has a system in place, but typically it's all stored in our minds.

As moms, we usually don't share responsibilities with anyone and take the "It's okay, I'll do it" approach. How does this help us as busy moms? Why do we continue to take more and more on when there are systems we can put in place so we don't have to do everything all of the time?

This is why I created the **Chaos Control System** to equip moms to create and implement simple systems and procedures to help the home run more smoothly saving time and sanity.

In this chapter, you will learn three new systems that will conquer the three C's: **Clothing**, **Cooking**, and **Clutter**. It's all about being proactive and not reactive to help keep the positive momentum going.

CLOTHING

As moms, we have all sent our children back to their rooms to change their outfits. It could be 104 degrees outside, and my five-year-old will come out in pants and a long-sleeved shirt layered with a hoodie. How many times have you scrambled in the morning to find that pair of polka dot socks because you forgot it was a crazy sock day at school? I know I was guilty of this!

The amount of time that is wasted on battling our children to change to an appropriate outfit or find those elusive socks adds up. Here is a simple system that you can implement once a week to save that time and free up your morning a bit.

For each child, use either a set of plastic stackable drawers or a hanging closet organizer with five sections. Label each drawer or space on the organizer with the days of the week beginning with Monday. Each Sunday evening, you can set out the clothing needed for the entire week at once. Look at the weather and the calendar of events (hello, crazy sock day!) for the week and put all of the clothing needed for each day in its designated drawer or section.

> **TIP:** Allow your child to help you pick out their clothes, so they feel like they have a say in what's being selected and are more likely to wear what's being chosen the day it is worn. Each morning, your child will know what to expect and know exactly what to wear, saving time and stress on both your morning routines.

COOKING

Making dinner can be time-consuming and stressful if you aren't one to meal prep beforehand. Some of us don't have the time to cook all of our protein ahead of time and store it for later in the week all labeled and organized. After a long day of work, the last thing you want to do is do laps around the kitchen gathering all of the items you need to make dinner.

Do you see yourselves? You make your way to the spice cabinet to grab your seasonings, then to the pantry to grab your dry ingredients, then to the refrigerator to get the chicken, but then you realize you didn't grab the garlic powder and you find yourself right back at the spice cabinet. How much time does this take you each night? More than you think. Here is a simple solution to get you to save time and steps in the kitchen.

Start with separating your groceries into each meal. You know, that one onion that you buy for that one dish, grab it and put it with the chicken and the three carrots that you will need to make it. Once your group all your ingredients into separate dishes, put them in their containers. Everything from the chicken to the spatula to the specific measurement of spices, into the bin they go. Find some containers that will fit in your refrigerator that are easy to take in and out.

Now that everything is together when you go to cook that meal, simply grab the container and start cooking. It's like those pre-packaged meals that arrive in the mail that has all of the ingredients measured out ahead of time so you can get to cooking. No more laps around the kitchen, just grab and go!

CLUTTER

With kids come toys, lots of toys! They typically show up in every room of the house making them all look like game rooms. Some of us hate to ask the kids to pick up their toys and put them away or, as I said earlier in the chapter, so we pick them up ourselves because it's easier. What if we made our rooms more functional for everyone?

As a parent, we all love functional storage, am I right? There is nothing better than an ottoman that you can store blankets and random stuff in. You most likely own a piece of furniture like this right now, but are you using it to your advantage? Every room in your house should have a functional storage piece. A shelf with cubes, a decorative basket, or a dresser with drawers. Be sure to have this item close to the entrance of the room.

There are two reasons why this makes sense.

1. When you walk into the room, the storage will be behind you. This allows you to walk into an open and clean space (like when guests come over and you tell them to "excuse the mess" due to the pile of toys in the corner).

2. When the kids are playing with toys in the room and it's time for them to tidy up, they can pick them up and place them in the storage on their way out of the room.

Fewer trips in and out of the room to clean saves you time and griping!

> **TIP**: Keep one bin in the main area of your home (mine is the kitchen) as the main hub for toys floating around the house. As you come across an item that belongs to your child, put it in this central bin and collect them throughout the day. Before bedtime, ask your child to "check the bin" for any of his or her belongings so they can take what's theirs and put it away where it belongs. This way you are still being a mom and picking up the house but allowing your child to contribute to the household tasks and take more off your plate.

Now that you have some systems in place, write them down! As parents, we enjoy time away from the house for a date night or spa day with the girls without stressing about the kids, and wondering if things are getting done the way we prefer. We make lists and leave instructions for the sitter or in-laws each time we leave the house.

What happens to that list once you come home? Does it get lost in the drawer or crumpled up and thrown in the trash? What happens the next time you go out? Most likely, the instructions have not changed, and you find yourself making the same list all over again. That's just more time wasted! What if you had a manual for your home with all of your systems and procedures laid out for anyone to read? Our cars, electronics, and board games all come with instructions, so why shouldn't our homes?

That's why I created the **Chaos Control System: Home Edition**. It's a standard operating procedure for everything you can think of in your home life. From wi-fi passwords to weekly chore charts, to important medical information about your family, it's all in there. You can input all the information digitally by making changes easily to keep your playbook up to date. Print what you need.

The **Family Playbook** is the tool every mother needs to save time and stress less when chaos ensues at home. Or, if you want to take a load off of your mind and provide a book that has everything "mom would do," you can grab your copy here at **www.chaosncookies.com** and download a FREE Pocket Playbook for you to get started. Add this tool to your toolbox, mom, and free yourself up to have more time for YOU!

ELIZABETH JACKS SCOTT

For my Eight Grandchildren

START WITH THE KNOWING

by *Elizabeth Jacks Scott, M.A, M.Div, MSW*

Knowing yourself is the beginning of all wisdom
—ARISTOTLE

JOURNEY TO SAFE HARBOR COURSES AND COACHING is dedicated to assisting families to come together and to nurture better relationships. Whether one feels distant from one's parents, estranged from one's children or just wishing that your relationships were more harmonious and nurturing, I am dedicated to teaching the new parenting paradigm, which is proving to be transformational to relationships within families.

I have a long list of credentials and experience but the most important thing you need to know about me is that I have changed my own relationships with my children. That's right, I can attest personally what a difference this new paradigm in parenting can make in your life. I would never have believed it if I had not experienced it myself. My children used to tell me how difficult I was, and now they seek me out and want me around.

This was such a powerful experience that I am dedicated to teaching this new paradigm of parenting to others. I have been working with groups of parents who have been reporting dramatic changes on the quality of the relationships with their children. It is truly gratifying to have a parent tell me that tension is leaving her household and that she is finding harmony instead.

If you must know about me, I am an author of a book about my change entitled *The Journey to Safe Harbor*, a certified parenting coach by the JAI Parenting Institute, previously a therapist for over two decades, an ordained interfaith minister, a grandmother with several degrees (MA, MDIV, MSW), but what I really want you to know is that what I am teaching will transform the relationships within your family.

So, how are your relationships? Let's say you have a preteen and you are continually getting into loggerheads with her or him. You ask them to clean their room and they don't so their room is always a mess. You ask them to do their homework, and they go on social media instead. Their grades have been going down. You confront your child and tell them you are cutting their allowance until their grades get better. Instead of cooperating, they yell at you and say you are the worst mother ever.

Sound familiar? Are you at your wit's end? Do you keep wondering if you have been too lenient and now should be stricter? Do you find yourself more and more stressed, can't sleep at night, and more irritable or short tempered? Do you wonder what is wrong with your child?

As you read this story, what is wrong with the picture? Where does one start to begin to repair the relationships in this household? This mother has been trying behavior modification techniques, and they have not been working. Her children are getting more rebellious, and the mother has increasing stress and is out of control of herself. Her emotional temperature has been rising, and it is only making the situation worse.

Where do we begin to help this household or any of number of households where the anger and conflicts are rising, where family dinners are scenes of tension and conflict, or where parents feel unappreciated for all they have done.

Parent-centric parenting will make a big difference in your household. In other words, parents need to understand themselves, what their stress points are, what their needs are, and what they need to do to calm themselves.

Parents need to take care of themselves. Once they can find peace in themselves, they can have the necessary space to see their child differently. Instead of seeing their child as a challenge and looking just at their behavior, they will have the space to look under the surface and be curious about what is bothering their child. What's happening in their life that is producing this behavior? How they can give this child unconditional love and the help they need?

There is a two-part solution. **First**, the parent needs to work on themselves to find their center of serenity and **second**, the parent needs to be curious about what is bothering the child by listening to them to try to understand them. This will lead to being there for them with love, which is what every person needs to thrive, feel safe, be seen, soothed and secure in their world.

Of course, it you are a family with severe mental, emotional, or physical needs, then you need to seek appropriate professional help for those needs. I am here to address those families that generally are okay but wish their relationships were better.

LET'S START WITH PART ONE: THE PARENT NEEDS TO WORK ON THEMSELVES.

Yes, good parenting has to be taught because we all tend to parent the way we have been parented, and it takes conscious work to change, but the results are worth all the effort.

Let's start out with what is a connected, loving family where one feels known, cared about, safe, seen, soothed, and loved. If you have this kind of family, you are blessed. If not, I imagine that you are wondering how you to get there. I would like to tell you my own story to illustrate my answer.

I have to tell you at the outset that working on one's self takes humility and courage, but it is worth it. In fact, it is what philosophers and religions have exhorted us to do, "above all else, to your own self be true." The second Commandment: "Love your neighbor as yourself." It often takes a lifetime to understand what is meant in the second Commandment, but I think it means self-love is the prerequisite for loving your neighbor. Or the love you find within yourself becomes the source for love of your neighbor. Carrying out this finding transforms lives and family relationships.

...the love you find within yourself becomes the
source for love of your neighbor.

There are many ways to work on one's self: meditation, therapy, nature walks, the arts, and of course, thinking and feeling. I have outlined below some steps to take to bring about change.

It is your emotional self that needs to be understood as the most important element to enable your change. Take time to figure out how you are feeling. Once you have tuned into your feelings, there are various methods to begin to change them.

- **UNDERSTAND YOUR FAMILY'S EMOTIONAL HISTORY.** What happened to you in your childhood? Exploring previous generations through genealogy and other historical resources can illuminate current emotions and spur healing.

- **FIND COMPASSION FOR YOURSELF.** If you do, you will find it for others. Picture yourself as a child and what you had to experience. Find love for that small child.

- **FIND PEACE WITH YOURSELF** through meditation or therapy. You are the one family member whose actions you control. Seek spiritual awakening. Embrace a universal spirit of religion that can ease your burden and put it in a larger perspective.

NOW, FOR PART TWO: THE PARENT NEEDS TO TUNE INTO THEIR CHILD'S TRUE

Approach your children in a spirit of reconciliation, forgiveness, compassion, and curiosity. Look at your child with fresh eyes, listen to them, and see who they are. Listen for their needs. Think about how you can soothe them, make them feel safe, be seen, feel secure, and give them what they need.

Do you know how to take care of yourself?

As you begin the first step of tuning into your own emotional self, it is helpful to learn about the kind of attachment you had with your own mother or primary caretaker.

If one had a mother with the kind of attachment that was passed down in my family, the children did not feel seen, or even safe or secure because our mother was doing the feeding but not the emotional caretaking. She was too hurt herself, filled with her own unhappiness to have space inside herself to see and soothe her children. Most babies with this kind of attachment withdraw. They cease to let their needs be known for they have learned that they will not be heard.

Since this was the kind of attachment I had with my own mother, I became a people pleaser, which meant I spent my time studying other people to try to figure out what I had to do to get the love I craved rather than an having any idea of who I was. It has taken many years to tune into my own self, but the rewards have been life transforming.

Another form of attachment is where the mother is erratic in her responses, so the baby never knows how she or he will be responded to. In that case, the baby becomes filled with fear and is always on edge, wondering what will happen next. Of course, there is much more to attachment theory, but that gives you an idea.

Knowledge of the self is always a blow to the ego. I went around thinking that I was this wonderful mother when really, my children had not found me loving. What did that mean? I had a lot of unresolved shame that made it nearly impossible for me to really listen to my children to be loving in the way that they needed love from me. I took care of them but had not listened or seen who they were. I didn't do those things because I had not learned to do them for myself.

We must learn to love ourselves to love another. I had been copying the way my mother had raised me—which is what we all do. Yes, we all raise our children the way we have been raised unless we go on a great journey of searching to understand ourselves and to change. In other words, as psychologists have expressed it for decades, to make the unconscious conscious.

Something happened to me along the way, I found the old adage came true for me. "He who seeks finds, he whom knocks the door will be opened unto you." I found when I was at the bottom of the pit of pain from my grief or of my old feelings of being unloved or unwanted, that love found me. Something opened in my soul which I didn't understand but I felt known, accepted, and loved unconditionally. If I had not experienced it, I could not be telling you it is true. I think this was a change in my brain where new connections were made.

"He who seeks finds, he whom knocks the door will be opened unto you."

HOW DO YOU CHANGE YOUR RELATIONSHIP WITH YOUR CHILDREN?

What happened as a result of all this work seemed like a miracle to me. I visited my daughter's home one day and was just sitting calmly in her living room enjoying watching my daughter and her children playing when out of the blue, my daughter said to me, "Mom, I suddenly realized that you have become a stance for unconditional love in my home and we want you around." I was taken by surprise with her comment.

My daughter was now perceiving me as the one who had ceased to be the needy one, always looking for others' approval, and had become a presence that was now better able to take in others because I had found my center.

Now there is an amazing thing that takes place when one is true to one's self; one can begin to actually see, hear, be present with, affirm and unite with others—in other words, be loving. Loving is then something that we are all called to learn in our lives—to make this journey home to ourselves and thus be freed and enabled to love others as we learn to love yourself.

Why is this process of feeling your own feelings so powerful? As you feel what is inside, you stop projecting it out on everyone else. You stop blaming everyone else and take responsibility for yourself. Your brain makes new connections to the decision-making part of your brain. What I learned is the truth of the statement: "A step to the outside is a step in the wrong direction."

"A step to the outside is a step in the wrong direction."

ACTION STEPS TO BE TAKEN

Take time every day to tune into yourself. What are you feeling? What do you need? What is happening in your own life? Take care of your own priorities and needs first and then look at your children with refreshed eyes to see what they are feeling and needing with compassion and love.

www.Journeytosafeharbor.com

Courses on parenting and coaching

Journey to Safe Harbor: Memoir of Three Generations, Self-love, Forgiveness, Reconnection, 2021.

ELIZABETH BENNETT

Some Passing Thoughts...

To Kids and Teenagers: Your parents don't always do what you think is best, but just know they are doing the best with what they know!

To Parents: Your kids are dying for you to show up for them. They are the most important people in your life. . . be courageous and be there for them. Just a reminder: work will never end and you might lose your kid in the meantime. It happens every day ~ don't let your kid be the next statistic.

BEYOND YELLING
ARE COURAGEOUS
CONVERSATIONS

by *Elizabeth Bennett*

ANGRY, SHORT-TEMPERED AND FRUSTRATED; parents are fighting with each other because they don't know how to deal with their teen's obnoxious and belligerent behavior. The teen's slamming doors, silent treatment or one-word answers, and my favorite, 'eye rolling' have been the typical responses to parent's seemingly harmless question of "How was your day?"

It's no wonder, as their teenager's hormones are raging, that the pressures of their life weigh heavily on their minds, hearts and of course, on their ego. As adults, we have little or no idea what they actually worry about, as we are quick to say "Don't worry about that" as our regular mantra to ease their so-called worries. Throughout my years as a school administrator, I have heard countless admissions of fear-generated worries from teens. Their expression of worry about things like, am I good enough, do I fit in, do I really have friends, am I wearing the right clothes, am I going to pass this test, this course or this year run through their minds. I'm not sure how to do this (whatever this is) and I'm afraid to ask for help, I'm getting bullied and I can't tell anyone in case they make it worse. They often say that nobody listens to them. My parents are fighting, and I don't know if anyone really cares. I hate my life.

Imagine carrying all those worries and so many more, and we just simply say "Oh, that's silly, stop worrying, it's okay," as if that magical phrase will somehow ease the pressure and make the worries of their teen disappear instantly. If it were that easy, shouldn't we be saying it to ourselves as well, to reduce our own fears? We really don't know that these are legitimate concerns until we actually talk about it to understand and hear their perspective. The underlying concerns are the ones that need to be fleshed out so that your teen can see alternative solutions or pathways to resolution for themselves and possibly with your help.

And we wonder why the second cause of death is suicide amongst teens. You're likely saying in your head that this couldn't happen to my kid, well I can assure you that is what some parents said who lost their kid to suicide.

A DAY IN THE LIFE OF A TEEN

On this day, you all sleep in. Chaos reigns immediately as you get up, get dressed and rush to get your child(ren) out of bed. You know that they don't move quickly, so on your way by the kitchen you yell at them to hurry.

You are hustling around the kitchen getting something to eat for everyone, making lunches and you say, "You're not wearing that are you?" as they grab a food item, shove it in their mouth, load up their backpack, grab their hoodie and rush out the door to catch their bus.

Getting on the bus and heading to their favorite seat in the back, there are kids standing, yelling and tossing things around and making way too much noise. The bus driver yells for everyone to sit and be quiet, which is a welcome relief for your kid and likely many others; who just want to get on with their day. The moments of quiet have begun to create calm after the frenzy at home. Suddenly, your teen gets hit on the side of the head with some kid's lunch bag, which they promptly throw back while they say some rude, crude and socially unacceptable words. And as your kid turns back to sit in their seat, they notice the bus driver is looking straight at them. Heading off the bus, your child notices that the bus driver is writing and sees their name on the top of the report. Walking to their locker, your child gets pushed and shoved in the overcrowded hallway while hearing teachers and the Vice Principal yelling at kids to hurry to class. Entering the class, your child notices that the desks, tables, and chairs have been moved and a new seating plan has been created. Your child finds a seat, and the kid who teases and bullies your kid sits right down beside them. The teacher is 'yelling' to get everyone settled to start the day, while asking for permission forms, assignments and reminders about upcoming tests and project dates. Meanwhile, the bully has whispered something to your teen, just loud enough for them to hear. Leaping out of their seat, your kid decks the bully, trying to get them to finally stop their harassment. As the teacher turns from speaking to another student, they yell out your child's name and tells them to go to the office.

THE DAY IS GETTING PROGRESSIVELY WORSE RATHER THAN IMPROVING.

At the principal's office, your teen describes the morning frenzy at home, the miserable bus ride, including being hit by some kid's lunch bag, the note to the office from the driver, the extra running and push-ups required before practice because they were late, and their coach hates it when people are late, the new seating plan in class and then how the bully was the icing on the cake. It wasn't even 9:30 in the morning, that's a lot for anyone, let alone a teenager.

With all of that happening for your teen, who likely doesn't have the skills and strategies to deal with it all, it's quite a lot to manage. As the principal calls you to inform you that your child will be suspended for fighting, their behavior becomes even more escalated, worrying about how you are going to react and what will happen when they arrive home.

You've now arrived at work, preparing for a presentation that you and your colleague are giving later in the day when you receive a call from your child's principal. You arrange to have your teen picked up when your colleague knocks at your door and indicates that the presentation has been moved up and is now due in an hour. You lose your shit at your colleague and then quickly apologize, explaining about the morning and what happened with your child. Your presentation starts and suddenly the connection is interrupted, and perhaps unnerved, you gather yourself and quickly regroup and adjust the presentation. Working with your team, you complete your presentation successfully, despite the internet glitch.

Finally, you get into your car at the end of your day of upheaval, turn on your radio to hear P!nk singing, "I've had a shi##y day, you've had a shi##y day" as you sing along and smile while shaking it off.

This is generally not the same for many teens. They feel alone and lonely, trying to make it through the day, fearful of being ridiculed by their peers, afraid to ask for assistance and working through the world of teen life by themselves while trying to do well in school and please their parents at the same time. It's a lot. For anyone.

You arrive home to find your child sprawled on the couch with their hood up and earbuds in. Walking over to them, you touch their knee to get their attention. You sit down, acknowledging that the day was not the best while asking them "What happened?" and letting them know that you are listening. You talk through the situation, re-affirming your love for your child and discussing a plan together of how to deal with the situations at school. Discussions about your child's altercation with the 'bully' are also part of the conversation with consequences that are appropriate and timely added to the mix.

In this scenario, the parent had a courageous conversation with their child.

Such is not always the case; oftentimes the child is isolated or sent to their room to figure it out by themselves, ridiculed and additionally punished while no new strategies are provided so that the child has the skills to deal more appropriately should a similar situation repeat itself.

This is where I come in, to help support you as a parent, as well as your teen to re connect and create a new relationship with courageous conversations. Here's what I know for certain —there many ways to communicate with your teen, ways that create connection rather than frustration, ways that build trust and improve relationships rather than create disconnect and more heartbreak. I can show you how. This is a space of perspectives, being curiously engaged and open to understanding versus judgment. A place where new and different questions, inquiries, respectful and responsible courageous conversations can occur that provide opportunities to create new, powerful and loving relationships with you and your teen.

Click the link below or enter the link into your browser to get my gift: *5 Strategies of Dedicated Listening*, and schedule a "Teen Strategy" call with me so we can work together to create a harmonic space for your teen, your family and for you. Visit me at **https://courageous-parents.com**

EDINA ADLER, LCSW

Dedicated to Rebecca and Jacob, now 20 and 18, and their father, my husband Brian, who have brought unexpected joys (and challenges) into my life. And with my utmost respect for all those who have loved and successfully raised children who were brought into their lives by a partner, and who gave their hearts to a stepchild in spite of the many challenges they were likely to face.

SUCCESSFUL STEPPARENTING: AN ACT OF LOVE—AND A TEST OF PATIENCE!

by *Edina Adler, LCSW*

NEARLY 13 YEARS AGO, I married a man with two adorable children, ages four and six. I was in my forties when I met my husband. I'd thought I'd never find someone to raise a family with, and I felt blessed to have these two children in my life. Less than a year later, when their mom lost custody to their dad, I became a full-time stepmom overnight. And overnight, I also discovered a whole world of conflict I hadn't known existed!

As a former social worker with foster youth, and a child custody and divorce mediator, I thought I could handle the most difficult family conflicts. Between the hostile behavior of my husband's ex, my stressful job as a social worker in child welfare, and my lack of preparation for being a stepparent, I began to get overwhelmed. We had child custody court hearings almost once a month for several years and spent many days in the county courthouse. I stopped doing things I loved in my now-non-existent spare time. After many nightmares about the ex breaking into the house, I convinced my husband to get a security system. That was a low point, but it got even worse. At work one day, I found myself sitting in my car in the parking lot of the Department of Family and Children's Services, hiding behind my tinted windows, screaming like a crazy person. I was starting to crack under the chronic pressure to be the perfect mom, wife, child welfare social worker... lamenting my failed efforts at trying to befriend the ex.

I realized that I needed to ask for help and started seeing an excellent therapist. I began to work on quelling my people-pleasing habits and started doing things I loved again—things which fed my soul, like art, writing, and reading for pleasure. I also cut down my work hours to a measly thirty-five instead of fifty-five or sixty. In less than a year, my life transformed; I no longer feared the ex, regained my sense of humor about children's behaviors, and felt hopeful and optimistic about our family again. I also discovered my struggles as a stepparent were very common. So, I decided to do something to help other stepparents, and I trained with the Stepfamily Foundation in NYC to be a Stepfamily Coach. A few years later, I was licensed as a therapist and trained in the Gottman Method for couples, along with several other modalities addressing attachment and trauma. My past training in drama and art therapy also became part of my approach.

Just as I struggled through both internal and external challenges, so have many of the parents and stepparents I work with. At times I didn't know how I'd get through it. Luckily, I had a lot of training prior to becoming a stepparent, and believe me, I used a lot of it! My husband has had full custody for over ten years now. His ex basically cut herself and her family off from her kids, and yet, the kids, now college age, are doing great. But it took some effort to get here.

I've learned that there are lots of wrong ways to do this, and it's the kids who suffer most when we make the wrong choices.

Parents need support when you bring together ex-spouses, multiple sets of parents, and children with divided loyalties. Luckily, I've discovered it is possible to have a family that lives in (mostly) harmony in spite of the fallout often caused by an unfriendly divorce.

Now I'm on a mission to help other stepfamilies and provide the kind of support that I wish I'd had at the beginning of my journey as a stepmom. I now know that even a difficult divorce can be managed to minimize the impact on the kids, and the chaos can be transformed so that everyone in the new family feels cherished and worthy. I'm here to tell you that stepparenting can be as rewarding as raising your own children if you know how to steer clear of the stepfamily minefields; with the right tools, you can save your sanity and relationship in the process.

LOVE IS LOVELIER THE SECOND TIME AROUND... ISN'T IT?

Many people believe second marriages are more likely to succeed due to lessons learned from the first marriage. My hope is that, after reading this chapter, you'll understand why that's not true, so you can avoid becoming part of that statistic. Sixty to seventy percent of couples with kids in second marriages will split up within two to four years, thus putting kids through another gut-wrenching experience.

SOME INTERESTING FACTS FROM THE PEW RESEARCH CENTER:

- 1 out of 3 children under 18 lives in a stepfamily.
- 42% of American adults have a close step relationship.

- 40% of American women will live in a stepfamily at some point.

Cohabitation without marriage is on the rise and has a higher failure rate than marriage. Divorce over age 50 doubled from 1990-2010, followed by recoupling a lot of the time. That means millions of children and teens are being impacted by their parents' failed relationships and the fallout of non-optimal co-parenting. But there are proven strategies to both eliminate the behaviors that undermine so many relationships and create stepfamily success/harmony.

As the founder of Step-by-Step Family Coaching, my goal is to help parents—whether biological or not—learn how to help their new families thrive and avoid the common pitfalls faced by a majority of parents raising kids with a partner who is not the biological parent.

I recently learned that in France, the term for what we in the U.S. call a "stepfamily" basically means the "reconstituted family," which is actually pretty accurate. This also partly explains why it's such a challenging experience. There are a lot of ways to get it wrong and wind up with a gooey mess!

I've worked with kids and families for over twenty-five years, started a non-profit serving at-risk youth, been a Family Court Mediator, and experienced ups and downs myself as a step-mom. I even took a detour into children's publishing and theatre. In other words, I've seen plenty of mistakes parents and stepparents can make, and also some fine models of parenting, in many different environments. But the worst and most damaging blunders are usually the ones made in a reconstituted family. That's because most people don't understand what is involved in reconstituting a family—what to say, or not to say, and how to avoid the landmines that can shatter a family, even when the second partnership feels so promising and full of love at the start.

IN MY 25+ YEARS OF WORKING WITH KIDS AND PARENTS, I CAME TO REALIZE A FEW THINGS:

1. Emotionally healthy kids don't happen by accident.
2. I didn't want my kids to spend their adult lives getting over their childhood (so I'd better learn a few things before I became a parent).

And most disturbingly/surprisingly:

3. There's very little support to deal with stepfamily dynamics. It's not taught in social work or psychology courses of any school I've attended.

That's why I created the Stepfamily Blueprint—a process to build parenting and partnership skills at the same time because it turns out that a strong partnership and effective parenting go hand-in-hand. And, surprise... it turns out marriage takes work—which includes working on yourself! Good parenting (and partnership) calls for understanding your own blind spots, what triggers you, how to exercise self-control when you want to say something out of hurt or anger, and how to be the best you even when you feel like letting your inner gremlins take over. In addition to those skills, I address the landmines that can sabotage stepfamilies unless you learn how to navigate or defuse them.

You might already know that everything you do as a parent matters—not just in the short term, but over the course of the entire life of your child (or stepchild). Let's take it a step further: what you do as a parent matters to the entire community or communities of which your child will be a part, as well as all the close relationships they will have and their children will have.

Nobody wants to cause more emotional wreckage for kids. Nobody wants their kids to spend years getting over their childhood. Yet, as I mentioned earlier in this chapter, out of ten couples who bring children into a second marriage or partnership, more than half of those couples will be picking up the pieces within two to five years. As a result, forty-five percent of those kids will be dealing with anxiety or depression for years afterward.

Let that sink in for a minute.

Considering this responsibility, doesn't it make sense that before anyone becomes a parent or stepparent, they should get at least a crash course to understand what goes on in a child's brain and how to cope when things don't go the way they'd like? You don't get behind the wheel of a car without some training, without passing a test, without someone getting you to at least consider the consequences of running a red light or driving under the influence. I'm not suggesting a car is like a human being. You don't trade up for a better model (though parents at times might wish they could). Well-meaning parents do, however, send their kids to therapy to be "fixed" when they themselves could use some "fixing."

From what I've seen in over twenty-five years of working with children and families, many of us have not prepared for this awesome, life-changing and future-impacting responsibility by getting some training. Yet, driving a car requires at least thirty hours of instruction in most states.

Unfortunately, the harm done by dysfunctional parenting is less visible to most people. A fact that deserves more attention is that kids in foster care (a system which I worked in for about five years) do not have good outcomes: forty-five percent of those kids who age out of foster care become homeless or are trafficked or worse. Roughly seventy-five percent of prison inmates have been in foster care for extended periods of time (i.e., have not received adequate parenting or love), and much of the addiction and crime that results from kids who grow up without hope, opportunity, or adequate empathy (due to a lack of attachment to a loving caregiver) is blamed on the "bad choices" they make, rather than on the root causes—poverty and poor or non-existent parenting (complicated by mental health and addiction).

What's a parent to do?

Aside from keeping kids out of the foster care system, there is much that parents (and stepparents) can do to ensure their kids are resilient and better able to cope with life's ups and downs.

The SEARCH institute, in its (c2006) study involving almost 150,000 students in grades 6-12, has identified forty positive experiences and qualities—called Developmental Assets™, which they organize into the following eight categories:

1. **Support** (having people who love, care for, accept, and appreciate them)

2. **Empowerment** (making kids feel safe, respected, and valued/valuable)

3. **Boundaries and Expectations** (reasonable ones)

4. **Constructive Use of Time** (giving kids opportunities to develop new skills and interests)

5. **Commitment to Learning** (valuing and encouraging it and building a child's confidence)

6. **Positive Values** (teaching guiding principles to help youth make healthy life choices)

7. **Social Competencies** (interacting and dealing with different people, making hard decisions involving others)

8. **Positive Identity** (belief in one's self-worth and a sense of agency/control over their lives)

A more detailed copy of this study is available from **www.search-institute.org**.

For stepfamilies in general, there are three major minefields, which can upend a partnership or marriage.

1. **UNREALISTIC AND UNHEALTHY EXPECTATIONS:** The belief that bonding will be quick, gratitude and/or respect from step kids will be forthcoming, and the Brady Bunch myth of a happy family as soon as everyone is together is unrealistic. The "happily ever after" takes time, and a Jekyll and Hyde effect is more likely if too much intimacy and togetherness is foisted upon the kids.

   It is much better to spend one-on-one time at first—parent/child, stepparent/stepchild, etc. There is a big misunderstanding regarding how differently stepfamilies function from biologically intact ones. The adjustment is harder for girls but especially girls in their early teen years.

2. **PARENTING STYLES THAT ARE IN CONFLICT:** A weak partnership or weak links in the relationship that have not been repaired will be worsened by the conflicts that step-kids and divorced co-parenting bring. A strong partnership and good communication skills—especially about parenting—help a couple weather the storms they will inevitably encounter as a stepfamily, particularly around discipline.

   A stepparent needs to be both loving and firm (aka authoritative parenting), setting limits appropriate to the child's maturity level while remaining empathic, nurturing, and responsive to the child's needs and feelings.

3. **LOYALTY CONFLICTS AND THE DYNAMICS OF DIVORCE:** Inner conflicts will exist within the children regarding their parents and stepparent(s) and within the adults regarding their kids and new partner. Kids will resent and/or ignore the stepparent who is taking away their parent's attention, and stepparents might resent their new partner's kids or even the ex for the demands of time and financial resources on their relationship. Children can pull a relationship apart if the couple has not developed a very strong foundation. Kids' feelings and the difficulty of the transition are not necessarily addressed, and the topic might even be avoided and treated as taboo On the flip side, parents may still be angry at their ex and say unflattering or even derogatory things about them just to "set the record straight." That's the last thing a kid needs, especially if they've just lost everything that was familiar to them—their family, home, and sometimes friends. Children are biologically wired to bond to their parents, and more inner turmoil is created by leading a child to feel their parent is not a good person or doesn't want to take care of them. If that's the case, the child will figure it out when they are old enough.

Stepparents are just as capable of providing these experiences which build resilience in kids. I'm also here to tell you, raising non-biological kids can be a very rewarding experience, with times that are magical, joyful, and loving. However, kids will not make your life magically better in every way, improve your finances (usually the opposite), give you more time to do the things you enjoy outside of parenting, or fix whatever's not right in your life. As a working stepmom, I've experienced both the joys and tribulations of parenting as a full-time stepparent for close to a decade, due to the bio-mom's absence.

I struggled through both internal and external challenges, and so have many of the parents and stepparents I work with. At times I didn't know how I'd get through it, and it took some effort to reach the other side. I believe all parents should take the time to get some training and support if they are going to take on the very important job of raising children, whether their own or their partner's.

LET ME ASK YOU A COUPLE OF QUESTIONS:

- Did you start your new family with high hopes but then found yourself exhausted from trying to please everyone?

- Do you sometimes end the day feeling like you're in a warzone, with fights almost every day?

- Do you have kids who are loyal to the biological parent and who treat you like their enemy? Or at best, like an outsider—and definitely not a parent figure, even if you are doing all a parent should do, providing the love, comfort, protection, guidance, and resources as if they were your biological children?

Trust me... been there done that and have the tee shirt and mug to prove it.

So now, I help divorced or separated parents and stepparents ensure that their next relationship is their "happily ever after." I believe in second chances at love. I feel privileged and honored to be able to do this work, and I've had a lot of success in the past ten years—over 80%—in keeping marriages together. I want you to know there are proven ways to prevent those landmines from exploding in your stepfamily so you can have a peaceful home, well-adjusted kids, and a great relationship!

I'd love to invite you to a free training I offer several times a year, called "More Love, Less Drama: How to Avoid the 3 Major Step-Parenting Minefields and Have Your Happily Ever After," where I share three keys to helping your second (or third) chance at love succeed.

PLEASE JOIN ME FOR THE NEXT WORKSHOP IN FALL OF 2022.

To sign up for my next free master class, please email me at **morelovinghome@yahoo.com** with subject: Masterclass - or check my website for updated information.

CLICK THIS LINK TO GET MY 10 SUCCESSFUL STRATEGIES FOR STEPPARENTS

https://successfulstrategiesforstepparents.now.site

I also have a checklist Help Your Kids Survive and Thrive Through Divorce and Remarriage

https://tipstocopewithdivorce.now.site

If you want to get in touch, please email me at **morelovinghome@yahoo.com**. Also, you can take the quiz on my website to see how you're doing with some of the major challenges of stepfamily life.

www.stepbystepfamilycoaching.com

DR. JJ KELLY

*To all those kids out there who just don't "fit in"....
stop trying. "Normal" doesn't exist and conformity
is boring. Be brave enough to discover and embrace
all the things about you the scared normies call
"weird." It's way more fun, honest, and less tiring
than pretending and self-betrayal. The world will
be a more colorful, joyful place when we all find our
courage to take on this quest. Get out there and BE
YOU! Xxjj*

PRACTICAL ADVICE FROM THE PUNK ROCK DOC

by *Dr. JJ Kelly*

WELL, HELLO THERE! Nice to meet 'cha, I'm Dr. J.J. Kelly—The Punk Rock Doc. I'm a licensed clinical psychologist and emotional intelligence skills training expert and consultant. If you have an unhappy kiddo, they work with me and they learn to like themselves again.

Period.

In the last 20 years, I can count on one hand the number of kids that **haven't** become noticeably happier after we've worked together. No shit. I'm the one the meds doc sends the kid to when they're cutting or acting out and have seen a bunch of other shrinks and they haven't improved a helluva lot. I lead with radical authenticity, embracing our "weird", humor, laughing, and play with zero bullshit. People of all ages have benefited from my one-of-a-kind approach to increasing overall quality of life and joy. But my faves are the adolescents—which I consider 10-years old thru thirty...ish.

I did individual psychotherapy, groups, psycho-education, lecturing, and dialectical behavior therapy (DBT) for fourteen years in group practice, another two in private practice, and decided a more effective way for me to work with participants (I don't say "patients" anymore) was to teach them a toolbox of emotional intelligence skills that they can use to improve their lives, and go out into the world without a dependency on me.

Our current mental health system is antiquated, full of "isms", expensive as hell, and from what I've seen... often ineffective. I think that's dumb. And I'm not gonna destroy my own self-esteem and self-confidence and power by taking money for shit that doesn't work... for YEARS. I also don't even wanna take the three grand a month from parents when what I do DOES work... for YEARS! So, I started my own company, teach the skills exclusively, teaching the advanced students to mentor.

We run what I refer to as emotions "camps." I write, podcast, interview, and make sure that the longer a student wants to learn from me, the less expensive it gets. Shit, once I get funding, I'll enthusiastically teach this in schools for nothin'. If yer down with this idea, donate and/or send high-rollers who are into mental health reform my way!

I work with the young folx, exclusively, so for you – the parents, I wrote the, *Holy Shit, My Kid Is Cutting* book. Whether your kid is self-harming or not (unfortunately they probably are, were, or will from what I've clinically seen), this book is a parenting manual. It's meant to supplement the fact that I don't do separate parent or family meetings with my course, and to help you, as parents, manage your own anxiety.

I think your fears are valid, I've just found that the kiddos won't tell me anything if they think I'm a narc. And you definitely WANT them to tell me everything so you have a skilled clinician's eyes on the whole situation. The cutting book supports your family's values and your ability to structure behaviors in alignment with those values.

Then, the *Holy Shit, I'm A Gifted "Misfit"* book – though written to your pre-teen, teen, or adult kid – IS my 8-week beginner course, in as thin a book as I could make it. This way, all parents know exactly what's being taught to their kid, without having to be directly involved in their work with me. Some parents like that. Some parents don't – they want direct involvement. Some programs involve the parents, and I respect that approach and see why it can work. Mine just isn't that kind of program. The choice is yours.

I have, recently, set up a once a month zoom call for parents that have read the cutting book. Obviously, it's better if they've read the *Gifted "Misfit"* one too, since it contains the skills taught, practiced, and that are positively impacting the students' lives. Many parents do end up reading (or listening to) the "misfits" book, which is helpful. Anyhoo, that monthly call is just a straight Q&A coaching call, and it is not for the faint of heart. I pull no punches. For some, it might be easier comin' from a male doc, but we're here to change those "isms," so... learn from my two decades of clinical edge and expertise or don't... up to you.

Ok! Now let's get to my take on the meat 'n potatoes of why we're here – the 3-steps of *No-Problem Parenting*™.

1. SEEK FIRST TO UNDERSTAND:

Why's yer kid cutting, self-harming, and/or acting out and why are you reacting the way you are to it? Well, shit... your reaction is easy to understand. Terror. Few things scare parents more than learning the kid they made is hurting themselves on purpose. But drugs and sexual acting out are just as scary—not to mention tanking grades and the appearance of unmanageable rage and/or total apathy.

The blood and physical evidence of self-harm sure as hell doesn't help anybody stay calm. I mean, I'M calm—cuz I understand it and have helped thousands of kids stop—but I can honestly say that I don't know how much that would even help if it was MY kid.

Which is why ya hand the kid off to a pro that knows what they're doing. Easier said than done, though. Most people with financial means, go to the perceived "top": A 60+ year old Harvard dude that gives 'em meds on a first meeting. Lemme tell you now: that's not always the best path for the kid.

Doctors are known for being terrible listeners. And doctoral and medical degrees are more a sign of privilege than intelligence—certainly emotional intelligence. It's such an illusion that our society still treats doctors like gods—I mean, I get it. When a person is scared, they often want someone to tell them what to do, but that off-load of responsibility can backfire pretty hard when your doc got all C's yet walks the earth like they have nothing yet to learn. Gods, we are not. We are people with expertise. If what we teach resonates with you, and matches your core values, and you feel the truth of it in yer gut, great! If not, throw the advice in the bin.

The answer to why your kid is cutting and/or acting out can be more complex. There are certainly individual differences which is why I ask questions and actively listen to your kid's responses, so I can learn about them and their values and unmet needs.

And just cuz they have unmet needs doesn't mean you fucked up. You're not expected to know everything and make no mistakes—you're a human being. So are they. Mistakes are part of the whole gig for all of us. And we're set up for missing out on emotional connections with each other because no one ever **TAUGHT** us anything actually useful about human emotions and how to effectively manage 'em.

THINK about that for a minute, dude! We are humans. Humans have emotions. Why wouldn't we want to learn an effective model for managing life's ups and downs and the emotions those events generate. If we **ALL** want to love and be loved and be happy, **WHY** has no one ever taught us the practical steps to achieve that?! That baffles and infuriates me on the daily, but that's what gives ME purpose: teach everyone that wants to feel more joy **HOW** to **FEEL MORE JOY!**... not perform or pretend joy— which is what most people are doing—but actually enjoy life most of their days. My goal is for everyone to reach their deathbed proud and ready.

So, in this case, you and I both need to manage any emotions we may be having about your kid's behavior and listen and learn what emotions are so big that they think they need to self-harm to manage 'em. My money's on anger... ineffectively managed rage. I haven't met a kid that self-harms that doesn't have unprocessed anger. It's not the only thing goin' on, but it IS usually in the mix. When we start our work together, some of that gets dispersed onto me—which is healthy—and also, you want a plan for how you want to behave when it starts coming out more with you. Which leads us to #2...

2. PREPARE FOR THE WORST.

I agree with *No-Problem Parenting*™ in that there **ARE** curveballs, and preparing for some things is just a sound plan. SO! My best advice for raising adolescents is get ahead of the crisis. Simply, get the kid in to see a professional at the first signs of trouble: skipping school/playing sick, grades slipping, they come home wasted or you find a vape, you see sexual content in texts... anything.

Prevention is largely achieved by getting the family on the same page right outta the womb, and it can be as simple as printing out a "Feelings Sheet" or "wheel" and practicing everybody saying how they feel instead of only what they **THINK**. I have a whole template in chapter 10 of the cutting book, with suggestions of a family contract with expectation and privileges and consequences. The problem is, of course, that family's only do this once the shit has hit the fan, so the kid(s) think of it as a punishment. Get ahead of that and just write one, as a family, as soon as they are school age—hell!... as soon as they're **BORN**! What could it hurt?!

And when they're approaching puberty, take a gander at YOUR teen years. What kinda trouble did you get into and what turned out ok and not okay. I don't know what the hell happens to people when they have kids?! It's like they contract total amnesia about the kind of shit teens get into—and not every goddamn thing came with a diagnosis or was life-threatening. I think the "amnesia" comes from not having the skills for effectively managing fear. Fear generates worry thoughts, and worry thoughts are often not fact. But who taught us that? No one.

Last thing is: you are not your kid's friend. You brought someone into the world, so do what's in **THEIR** best interest. Sometimes that means "being the bad guy." If you're too fragile to have them pissed at you, don't have kids. It's perfectly normal for teens to be pissed at their parents, and I would argue, clinically, it's healthier than guilt and shame—which comes from protecting your ego and thinking they are responsible for managing your feelings. Don't be that parent. We got enough of 'em already. It's where the word "snowflake" came from. It's just mistakenly put on the kids, not their parents — whom they learned it from.

3. CHANGE THE CONVERSATION:

No-Problem Parents lead with empathy, understanding, and guidance. Although I'm a little more hardcore than *No-Problem Parenting*™, we definitely agree on empathic (yes, the clinical word is "empathic", not "empathetic") communication. A core tenet and practice of my skills training is validation. Validation is at the core of Dr. Lenihan's dialectical behavior therapy (DBT), and she based it on Thich Nhat Hahn's Miracle of Mindfulness, which is basic Buddhist teachings.

The way I teach this is that we validate all emotions, and not all thoughts and behaviors. You can validate your kid's emotional experience without agreeing with them. "You're obviously hurt" is something you can say when your kid's "in a fight" with their best friend. That would be meeting them where they are, emotionally, without agreeing or saying the classic, "You'll be friends again next week."

You probably aren't wrong, but right or wrong is not what it's about. It's about communicating in a way that creates connection and makes your kid want to talk to you. You're behaving in a way that conveys respect and caring instead of minimization and dismissal. We wanna treat people the way we want to be treated.

More importantly, you are modeling compassionate behavior and confident, caring, connection. They are watching you— even when they pretend, they aren't or they "don't care." And they want your love and approval so, so much. So, teach 'em! Learn to laugh at yourself, and de-stress by not taking yourself too seriously.

Apologize when you make a mistake—most parents fear it will undermine their authority. In fact, it strengthens it. Plus, you're teaching your kid a life lesson: what I call, "eating your shit sandwich with dignity." A real apology clears out shame. A bullshit apology: "I'm sorry YOU (or but)..." creates shame. Shame erodes self-esteem and self-confidence. And hiding from it or pretending shame is not there creates fear and anxiety. Actively model behaviors that match your values, and you will teach your kid to do the same. And that **BUILDS** self-confidence – which is what you ultimately want for them anyway. It's a lifelong practice. And it works.

So, what can you do right now? Today?! Go to **drjjkelly.com** and print out a "Feelings Sheet", put it on the fridge and start practicing naming (**VALIDATING**) emotions in your family. If you're gonna print one out from the internet, make sure that list doesn't have thoughts masquerading as emotions (it def will, so just cross 'em out).

That's so common now: people tryin' to pass off thoughts as emotions, as though it makes them appear more evolved and in touch with their psyche (eye roll). I get, "I feel attacked" a whole lot, since my job is to challenge people's bullshit stories that negatively affect their lives. I usually just say, "attacked isn't a feeling. If you **THINK** I'm attacking you, how would you feel?"

Most people get it when I say that, but the reasoning is: Feelings are valid and true. Thoughts are opinions, guesses, assumptions, not fact, and, therefore, subject to respectful disagreement. (Reasonable people can still disagree, despite the sociopolitical climate of our country these days). You can only decide I'm "attacking" if I confirm my intention (or if I physically come at you, which still is not an emotion). You can guess at my intention, but then you gotta own that it's a guess, an opinion... not fact.

If you **FEEL** defensive or scared or worried or pissed when I challenge you, I have no argument with that. Your feelings are your feelings—they're valid. And we can talk that out. I probably said something someone else in your past has said to you and, therefore, what I said was a "trigger" of emotions related to your past. You are responsible for your triggers—not I. Yet, I'm a shrink, so it's worth talking out so I can teach you something about your reactions, feelings, and behaviors. Ya dig? Or maybe I was wrong, misunderstood, or was curt—in which case, I have an opportunity to model a rock-solid and sincere apology. Win-win.

Just listen to my books. Or check out all the free stuff on You Tube or Instagram: **drjjkelly**. The free consult for the courses, the monthly parent coaching call subscription, is on the website: **drjjkelly.com**. And you can always just call or text my work number: **510.595.7594**. I pretty much guarantee ya a laugh on any one of these platforms. And I sincerely believe it's laughter that helps the much-needed medicine go down. My very best to you in your quest to health and happiness. We're all in it together. Xxjj

DENISE SCHWENDEMAN

To Victoria & Luke - who continue to inspire me to always be the best version of myself. Thank you for choosing me as your mom. Love you both so much.

NATURAL SOLUTIONS
FOR UNWANTED STRESS

by *Denise Schwendeman*

JUST AS THEY HAVE BEEN USED for thousands of years, through wealthy dynasties and revered kings and queens, essential oils are still nature's most natural remedies. In ancient times, aromatic or essential oils were used every day and were a symbol of a person's wealth or status. Ancient Egyptians are believed to have used aromatic oils as early as 4500BCE, with traditional Chinese and Indian medicine following closely behind at between 3000 and 2000 BCE (1). These two well-known and highly regarded cultures recorded more than 700 medicinal substances, many of which we still use today, such as ginger, myrrh, cinnamon and sandalwood.

These volatile compounds distilled from plants as essential oils can be used today to provide effective and safe solutions to health challenges and goals. They are especially helpful in managing our reactions to everyday stressful situations.

My family has been using essential oils for 17 years and I have been educating others about the benefits of essential oils for over 15 years. Choosing to share these natural tools comes from the profound benefits we experienced, as a family, by using these amazing gifts of the earth. Essential oils empowered me as a mom, when I was desperately looking for answers.

I believe as parents we develop a "parental intuition" which probably comes from the thousands of hours that we've spent with and watching our children since birth! At every age we continuously look for signs and cues that alert us to how they're handling the myriad of changes and challenges in their lives. Armed with this knowledge we can discern whether our child is hurting physically, mentally, or is in harm's way.

My son Luke was born in 2000. It was a fantastic time! He and his older sister were a joy to watch as they were growing and figuring out their world. At just a few months old I noticed that Luke was having trouble digesting food, that he was only comfortable sleeping upright in his car seat and that there was bruising over his left eye. Deep inside I knew something was very wrong. Let's call it mother's intuition.

I made an appointment to see his pediatrician. It was his 4-month-old checkup, and the doctor wasn't overly worried about any of my concerns. The following week the issues remained the same. I called the doctor's office to be told not to worry that he'd grow out of it.

Two weeks after that, I noticed the bruising had spread to the other eye. Knowing that bruising doesn't spread like that, I brought him back to the doctor. Without too much more information, the doctor was ready to send us home again, but I pressed him by asking about the "rings" around Luke's eyes. It was then I saw a flash of recognition in the doctor's eyes, and he asked to check one more thing. He pushed on a couple of areas around Luke's belly and that's when he found the first tumor. Thus began a 10-year health journey. Luke is our two-time cancer survivor!

I share this personal story with you to reinforce your belief as a parent that you know your child better than anyone else and that you are—without a doubt—their best advocate.

When your child is in trouble, physically or mentally, the best outcome is always working hand in hand with trained professionals. For Luke's care, we were blessed with some of the best physicians, nurses, and specialists in the world. We worked very closely with them to make sure they were doing what they could for him without over treating him. He was so young.

We integrated many natural healing modalities to support Luke's good health such as Yoga, Meditation, Chiropractic care, Physical Therapy, Acupuncture, Karate, Shin Jun Jitsu, and Naturopathy.

Throughout Luke's journey, essential oils stood out as a tool that brought relief quickly, so we intentionally added them into our daily wellness routine. We used them to calm his worries and fears, to support his digestive system when taxed, to relieve head tension and discomfort throughout his body, and to help him get the rest he needed to heal physically, mentally, and emotionally.

Taking the time to lovingly apply oils to the bottoms of his feet or down his spine not only provided many health benefits, but it was also a wonderful way to bond with him. I highly suggest applying the oils in this manner with your children to deepen your relationship with them—especially when they aren't feeling well.

We diffused oils aromatically **A LOT**! He was (and still is) in charge of picking the oils to diffuse in the house. We made it fun—he could pick his favorite bottle of oil, or he could make his own blend—a science project he always enjoyed!

Today Luke also shares the many benefits he receives from essential oils with his friends to help them to manage their daily challenges more effectively.

Stress is pervasive and inevitable in our lives no matter how young we are. When we model coping skills and use tools, our children can learn from us to manage stress before it becomes harmful and habitual.

There are many stressors in our children's lives. They're exposed to so much more than we ever were. The unsettling times we're living through right now are difficult for adults to understand and manage and we have so much more experience than our children. These times can be deeply upsetting to our children. As a parent or care giver, we must take this opportunity to let them know that there are positive ways to manage their stress, worries and fears and that they can adapt and achieve a balanced state easily and naturally.

Our kids are always watching us for cues on how they should react in different situations. When we use tools to get ourselves into the right frame of mind before responding to a stressful situation or to our children, we can display appropriate behaviors for them to use as good examples.

Pure essential oils are great tools to calm, balance, and uplift our mood and the energy of a room. I recommend "the oxygen mask," approach—meaning take care of yourself first. You can use essential oils to gain better control of your day too. Simply diffusing, inhaling or applying essential oils can be helpful in creating an atmosphere and opportunity for more positive interactions with your children. The ease of use and effectiveness of having these tools right in your home will be felt by all.

Essential oils don't always have the same impact on every person because we each have unique chemistries. Involving your child early on in choosing which essential oils they prefer is the best way to introduce the oils to them. Allowing them to find the ones that support them best is part of the journey. When they take ownership of which oils are selected, they are much more likely to use them.

Make it easy and fun for them to use oils. Place a small tray with 3 or 4 choices next to the diffuser and put your child in charge of deciding which oil to diffuse. If you have more than one child, let them take turns.

It's the parent's job to empty the diffuser out at the end of the day.

SO, WHAT EXACTLY ARE ESSENTIAL OILS? They are natural extracts steam distilled or pressed from herbs and plants. They work in our bodies the same way they work in plants—they provide nature's defense. The natural chemical properties in these pure oils support our well-being. Just as we receive health benefits from eating the plants themselves, we can receive health benefits from inhaling, applying and ingesting pure essential oils.

Essential oils are highly concentrated and potent. They are 50 to 70 times more powerful than herbs. An example of this is that one drop of peppermint is equal to 28 cups of peppermint tea!

It's important to note that not all brands of essential oils are created equal. Please do your own research. The best oils to assist in supporting your health must be 100% plant derived (from the leaves, bark, stems or petals), certified pure, and tested to ensure there are no additives, no synthetics or harmful chemicals such as pesticides. Also, it is helpful to know where the plant is originally grown. The most diverse and beneficial chemical profiles come from plants grown in their indigenous habitat, in nutrient rich soil, at the right altitude and receiving the correct amount of sunlight and water.

WHAT'S THE DEAL ON DIFFUSING? Essential oils contain chemical constituents studied and known to assist in calming our nervous system. Inhaling essential oil aromas is the fastest way to access and trigger sense memories and emotions.

We can use essential oils to imprint and reinforce feelings you want to reach in your mind by connecting an oil of choice with the feeling you want to achieve. By repeating this connection out loud or simply thinking about it as you apply or diffuse the oil, your bond with this particular oil will grow over time and will remain, making this an excellent tool for you to restore balance quickly and effectively in many different situations.

EXAMPLE: "I like inhaling Melissa oil (or applying it to my wrists and over my heart) when I'm going into a new situation—it helps to calm me and feel more in control."

Diffuse in the morning to gently set a positive mood for the day. When you return home or while your children are studying, diffuse to boost their immunity and to wake up their brain, making it easier for them to focus and concentrate.

As a family, one of our favorite times to diffuse is at night to help everyone relax, unwind from the long day, and to get our bodies in a calm state as we get ready for a good night's rest.

Another recommendation is to add a couple drops of your favorite calming oil to Epsom salts and then add to your bath water. This calms your nervous system and sets you up for a good night's restorative sleep that is crucial to your overall good health.

WHY APPLY? Applying oils to your skin allows the oils enter your bloodstream in seconds and reach every cell in your body in minutes for whole body benefits.

Because the oils are so potent, I like to add a couple drops of a carrier oil to the essential oil when applying. I use a fractionated coconut oil because it's a medium weight and goes into our skin instead of sitting on top. Not only is this super effective in getting the oils into our bodies, it's also a lot less greasy!

Apply before going into a potentially upsetting situation or at the first sign of distress. The beauty of the oils is that you can support your body before you spiral all the way down. There is no reason to suffer an uncomfortable feeling until you hit bottom, start using them immediately when you begin to feel worried, fearful or upset in any way to stop the free fall of emotions. It's always easier to get back to balance if you're starting from a mid-way point.

Begin and end your day with the oils that support how you want to feel. Habit stack by using the oils to connect to a habit that you already have in your daily routine, like next to your toothbrush or on your nightstand. This will serve as a reminder to use the oil until it becomes its own habit.

Carry your oils with you in your knapsack, purse, pocket or sports duffle when you're headed into a new situation or a familiar situation that has the potential to upset you. Apply or inhale ahead of time and reapply as needed throughout the day.

Apply oils to your pulse points like perfume or cologne onto your wrists, temples, back of neck, top of head, spine, stomach and bottom of feet 2-3 times throughout the day.

SOME FAVORITES, MOST USED AND WELL TESTED OILS FOR MANAGING STRESS, BALANCING AND UPLIFTING OUR MOODS ARE:

FLORALS: Lavender, Roman chamomile, Ylang Ylang, Helichrysum, Rose

TREES: Frankincense, Cedarwood, Sandalwood, Vetiver, Copaiba

CITRUS: Lime, Wild Orange, Bergamot, Grapefruit, Green Mandarin

MINTS: Melissa, Peppermint, Spearmint, Rosemary,

SPICE: Clove

GRASS: Lemongrass

Top Choices in our household to calm racing thoughts and pulse are Melissa, Frankincense, Lavender, Lime, Cedarwood, and Bergamot.

As mentioned earlier, essential oils have been used for thousands of years as powerful tools for their healing properties. I hope you will embrace these natural tools to help support you and your loved ones in your daily lives. Remember it's not about which oil is right or what's the exact way to use them. It's about getting them on your body and inhaling them multiple times a day to receive their calming and uplifting benefits.

My wish is that you investigate the benefits of essential oils as a tool to help quickly reframe any upset and restore balance to your lives.

Thank you for reading this chapter. It's been my honor to share a little about the power essential oils with you. For a Free Balancing and Uplifting Our Minds & Mood with Essential Oils eBook or if you'd like assistance with your essential oil journey, please contact me at **dschwendeman@mac.com.**

https://linktr.ee/denisepolicanoschwendeman

References:

1. ncbi.nim.nih.gov (Biomed Research International) An overview of the biological effects of some Mediterranean Essential Oils on Human Health.

CURT JORDAN

This chapter goes to all the mothers and fathers who are brave enough to allow their children the freedom to play.

LET KIDS PLAY THEIR WAY

ELSE THEY LIVE IN YOUR BASEMENT FOREVER

by *Curt Jordan*

> "Prepare your child for the road,
> NOT the road for your child."
> —UNKNOWN

OBSTACLES WILL GET IN THEIR WAY, your children will get injured, have their feelings hurt, experience suffering and pain, and there is nothing you can do to stop this from happening; nothing. But we can prepare them for these experiences so they can learn the skills they need to lead happy and fulfilled lives. That is in essence what parenting is. Everything we protect our children from, we do not prepare them for; and everything we prepare our children for, they don't need to be protected from. As parents, our job is to slowly move our children from 100% protection to 100% preparation, and we do so as much as our children can tolerate. There are many ways to do this and, in my decades as a teacher, I believe the best, most natural, and effective way to prepare our children is through play. That is why I will teach you about Developmental Risk Play. What it is, why it's a need, and tools you can use to guide responsible decision making for your kids while helping you feel more comfortable in the process.

My name is Curt Jordan and I'm the Founder and Chairman of Kong Academy; a play-based education company that develops social and emotional skills through play and movement. My mission is to empower kids and parents with the tools they need to thrive in the world. I have witnessed that when kids are challenged, they find what they are truly capable of. They become stronger, wiser, and braver and I believe those kids are the ones that can lead and better the world. So, I want to share with you the resources I have developed from decades of teaching, so that I can help you guide your kids to become kinder and more independent people.

Kong Academy has impacted the lives of well over 10,000 kids and families., We have been in over 50 schools in the Seattle area, giving back with over 1,000 donation- based community classes. We have been featured in National Geographic, on FOX and ABC news, and won of the "Best of 2020 and 2021" award for being the best kids movement program in the country. I say all this because I want you to know, that what I'm about to share is not my personal opinion. It works! And it is my pleasure to share with you what you can do now to help your child grow up prepared for the world.

So, What are the things your kids do that make you gasp? The things your kids do that freak you out? Is it tree climbing? Jumping off of things? Rough housing in the living room? Is it when they are on the playground? Just take a moment and think of a couple of things your kids do that make you freak out.

Those things are called **RISK PLAY**, and Risk Play is defined as thrilling and challenging forms of play that involve a risk of physical injury (Sandseter, 2007).There are two 2 components to this:

1. The risky play has real risk of injury
2. The risk play is chosen by the child.

Why would I want my child to do these things? This may seem as if this goes against our desires to have our children grow up in a safe environment. But the reality is, this type of play is a natural and healthy developmental **NEED** in a child's life. To engage in play that is difficult, scary, challenging, and ultimately risky, will cause kids to become safer, healthier, and to develop needed the physical, social, and emotional skills that they will require to become independent. Sadly, kids are being given these opportunities less and less.

Through risky play, kids learn to manage their emotions and social interactions. According to the emotion regulation theory of play—one of play's major functions is to teach young mammals how to regulate fear and anger. In risky play, young mammals expose themselves to manageable amounts of fear where they learn to overcome it. In rough and tumble play, they may experience anger, as one player may accidentally hurt another. But to continue playing, to continue the fun, they must learn to negotiate conflict, overcome their anger, deescalate, or practice forgiveness. Thus, through play, young mammals learn to control their emotions and practice social situations that they will need throughout life. Kids who engage in Risk Play also develop **Responsible Decision Making Skills.**

Psychologists have shown that kids who engage in risky play are actually less likely to become injured because they're more adept at observing their surroundings and making responsible decisions. Interviews with children have shown that children engage in risky play to experience positive emotions such as fun, enjoyment, thrill, pride, and self-confidence (Coster &

Gleeve, 2008). And if you want your child to move, the surest way to avoid a sedentary child is to make sure that they understand, from an early age, that doing physical things is fun. Kids who engage in risky play are more active and tend to remain more active. They grow stronger, increase coordination, and improve cardiovascular health. Their vestibular systems are more challenged and, as a result kids improve their balance, eye position, posture, and attention, which results in less fidgeting behavior, and a greater capacity for concentration.

"Taking risks and succeeding can motivate children to seek further achievements. Builds: confidence, physical skills, social skills, adaptability, and independence. Failing can lead to testing new ideas, and finding personal capabilities and limits. In this way, children can overcome fears and build new skills."

Childhood development skills are learned through risky play; such as confidence, persistence, social skills, adaptability, and ultimately independence; Kids who are deprived of this experience suffer lifelong consequences. Adults often keep kids from taking part in these experiences. Adults often treat kids as if they were fragile. Our kids are not fragile. Fragile things break when they are stressed.

Children are antifragile. They need to be challenged to become prepared. Like the immune system, muscles, or bones, our kids become more prepared the more they are challenged within their capacity to build their independence. Independence does not happen with age. I, it happens through experience. Children do not learn responsible decision- making skills without the opportunity to make decisions. And play is how a child learns and explores the world.

Have I convinced you? Ok, so we know the reason for why it's a really good idea for kids to go out and engage in this type of play, but what can we do to help our kids stay safer and help us feel better when we see our kids doing this stuff?

First, we need to talk with our kids and teach them what a risk is. A risk is something that can be identified and chosen to participate in. Risk management is healthy, and an important part of growing up. But there are different kinds of risks. There are calculated risks: a risk that you take after carefully considering the possible results. And there is a reckless risk: a risk that you take without thinking or caring about the consequences. If we are to help children learn how to only engage in calculated risks, it will help to teach them a simple process they can use to make more responsible decisions. That is why I created the Risk Plan Method.

The **Risk Plan Method** is a 2-step process for making a calculated risk. What are the Risks and what is your Plan? Simple, right!? That's why it's easy to remember and to implement. When you ask your child what is the risk, you are asking them to investigate. Are the structures slippery? Wobbly? Is there something unknown they could get hurt on? How are they feeling internally about challenging themselves? Are they giving into social pressure? All summed up into two one questions: "What's the risk?" Then "What's your plan?" When asking these questions, you are asking them to create a solution that helps them take a calculated risk. Should they start with something easier? Should they test it somehow? What is a way they can make the risk a little less risky? Making a Risk Plan will take practice, but the more they use this system, the more they will begin to internalize how to progress safely. Be patient and consistent and you will see a huge positive change in their ability to make responsible decisions.

When introducing this concept, a conversation between you and your children can be extremely helpful when explaining what Risk is and making a Risk Plan. Create buy in with your child by making a promise and here's a script that may be helpful to guide this conversation:

"When you make a risk plan and talk to me about it, I will feel a lot safer about you playing the ways you like to." Is that something that you would be able and willing to do? Do you have any questions?" then let's make a promise..."

KID PROMISE: I promise to make and tell you my risk plan before I do something risky.

PARENT PROMISE: I promise to give you the time, space, and freedom to let you Play if you tell me a good risk plan and only stop you if I think something is wrong or you need help.

But what happens when we are out in the park, what exactly are you supposed to do when you see them engage in risky play that is outside your comfort level or their skill level? Ask yourself is this your fear or their limitation? If you find it's your fear that is the cause of the uncomfortable feelings, then focus on managing your own emotions instead of trying to control someone else's behavior.

SO, WHAT EXACT STEPS CAN WE TAKE TO KEEP THEM SAFE AND US FROM FREAKING OUT?

1. **COUNT TO TEN**: before you say something (or any manageable number) and during that time see how your child is handling the risk before intervening.

2. **ASK "DID YOU NOTICE?"** If you know they are capable and you have a concern, ask... "did you notice?" E.G: Did you notice the wood is really slippery from the rain? Did you notice the sprinkler sticking out of the ground right there? This creates mindfulness, and that is the first step towards kids making their own responsible decisions.

3. **PLAY WITH THEM,** often we lose our connection to what we are capable of and pass that on to our kids because we see what they are doing from our perspective and can't imagine having to do that ourselves. Then you begin to redevelop that connection to risk play and it will become easier for you to understand.

4. **BE CLOSE AND PREPARED:** Maybe they need help getting down out of a tree limb or they fall and need a bandage. Having first aid kits in the car, purse, or house, and knowing how to use them can cause create a lot of comfort because you will have a plan should something go wrong.

5. **LASTLY, DON'T WATCH:** Remember you probably got to run around unsupervised by adults and you're still here. Children have done so for thousands of years. There's no reason to punish yourself by forcing yourself to watch, if you really need to do not watch but be close by.

I know that this is a lot packed into a small chapter, but sincerely, thank you. Reading this is a testament that you are being the best parent possible by taking time to become more educated, and that you are willing for your kids to grow even when you feel uncomfortable. That means you are an awesome mom or dad! Not all moms and dads get to hear that enough, and I'm grateful for getting to share this with you. Thank you.

If you want to learn more about how to create a thriving parenting life, give your kids life-changing experiences, or want to learn more about Kong Academy, then please check us out at **www.kongacademy.org**

CHRIS LARSEN

This chapter is dedicated to my parents who taught me through practice, or just inspiration how to handle money. Also, I'd like to thank Clint Provenza, a dear family friend, for introducing me to both cycling and finance; two passions of my life.

HOW TO TEACH YOUR CHILDREN TO BE MONEY PROS

by *Chris Larsen*

MY FAMILY lives in Asheville, NC, home of The Biltmore, which was built by George Vanderbilt. When Cornelius Vanderbilt passed away in 1877, after building a transportation empire, he left $95M to his oldest son. In today's dollars, this would be over $2B. After his oldest son doubled this over the ensuing 10 years, his children spent almost all of it . . .

"This fabled golden era, this special world of luxury and privilege that the Vanderbilts created, lasted but a brief moment. Within thirty years after the death of the Commodore Vanderbilt in 1877, no member of his family was among the richest people in the United States. When 120 of the Commodore's descendants gathered at Vanderbilt University in 1973 for the first family reunion, there was not a millionaire among them."
— EXCERPT FROM "FORTUNE'S CHILDREN: THE FALL OF THE HOUSE OF VANDERBILT"

When we grow up, most of us are taught to "go to school, get good grades, go to college, and get a good job." Like a lot of eventual high-income earners, grade school was easy for me. I got good grades, tested well, was particularly good at math, and loved science. My family would say, "You'll be an engineer like your grandfather!" My grandfather was laid off and retired early at age 55, not because he wasn't good at what he did, but because he didn't want to play politics at work. Seeing this shaped my thinking from an early age as I realized a high-income job alone doesn't guarantee wealth building, financial independence, or the freedom to live on your own terms that comes with it. My family didn't teach me how to be wealthy.

I grew up in a firmly middle-class neighbor just south of Baltimore, Maryland, where my great grandparents had a vegetable farm. My father was from a family of dairy farmers in Wisconsin and was an entrepreneur who loved to enjoy life. Unfortunately, I never got to know him; just after I turned five, he tragically died when the engine of his plane failed over Lake Michigan during a trip to visit his parents.

The family went on Social Security, we ate food out of cans, my grandmother made my clothes and my mother stepped into the role of the sole caregiver. Ultimately, she married my stepfather who became a father figure in my life as we got back on our feet. He was a contractor who built houses and specialized in remodeling high-end homes around Annapolis, Maryland late in his career. During the late 1980s and early 90s, real estate was booming thanks to the Baby Boomers and their household-forming years. They were buying homes at a record pace. Builders and banks could hardly keep up. Remember Jimmy Dean sausage? Well, Jimmy Dean had a construction company called J.D. Construction that was building neighborhoods near our hometown at that time. Both my parents went to work for J.D. Construction. Things seemed pretty great until the Savings

& Loan Crisis. The housing market dried up, and they both lost their jobs as the company downsized.

Watching this process left an impact on me as I look back. I knew I didn't want to be in a position to lose my job. Whether it was genetics or due to my environment, I started my entrepreneurial streak at an early age. I never got a minimum-wage job like my friends. Instead, I rented out my video games, had a paper route, and did landscaping on the weekends in the local upscale communities where my stepfather would often do jobs. Once I started racing my bike as a freshman in high school, I began to spend my afternoons training and weekends racing and I'd make as much as $500 in prize money some weekends. I learned that there were better ways to make money than working a "9 to 5."

After grade school, I entered the Biomechanical Engineering program at Virginia Tech. The first weekend before school I joined the Virginia Tech cycling team. All I wanted to do at that point was race my bike. Life was great in college—going to class, training, and racing. Then, disaster struck when my best friend and training partner, Chris Strader, died of a brain hemorrhage the summer between my freshman and sophomore years. I lost my best friend, roommate, and training partner. I vowed to never let an opportunity pass me by again as I felt like I owed it to the world to live two full lives now.

I knew at this point that I didn't want to be an engineer and I decided that there was more to life than racing bicycles. I wanted and needed freedom to live life on my own terms. I loved the freedom of racing my bike and knew that I couldn't be an engineer working in a cubicle. A good family friend (the same one that introduced me to cycling) gave me an issue of Money magazine that illustrated the power of compound interest. I'll never forget the "aha moment" that inspired me. I opened a brokerage account and in the fall of 1998, began day trading, but ultimately settled on real estate as my preferred strategy. I bought my first property at age 21 and made plans to be financially independent by 40 years old.

Today, after realizing my goal of financial independence, I strive to help others do the same at **NEXT-LEVEL INCOME**. We help others achieve **Financial Independence** through education and investment opportunities. A big part of this is helping our next generation become financially literate and passing on the knowledge and habits that the wealthy and their families know.

Most of us are never taught about money. It's taboo. We don't talk about how much we make, how to invest and even the media vilifies the "rich." When the government tells you that if you make $400,000, you are "rich" and need to "pay your fair" share, it becomes deeply embedded in society. You might not feel bad for the surgeon making $400,000, living in California, paying a third of their income in taxes, but with a typical mortgage, tuition and some retirement savings, this family seems pretty middle-class.

The fact of the matter is that entrepreneurs and highly paid professionals like doctors provide jobs, give much to charity and pay the majority of taxes. Is it any wonder that our children not only are confused about money, but may even shy away from it?

As parents, we need to develop a healthy relationship with money. This is no different than if you don't have a healthy relationship with your spouse; it's going to be harder to teach your children how to have healthy relationships. I understand that not all of us have the privilege of being raised by both biological parents in an affluent, supportive community. I certainly didn't have all the advantages growing up. But I'm striving to give them to my two boys and teach them how to be truly wealthy. Not only financially, but also how to enjoy the life that they choose to live.

How can we best teach our children about the true value of money and how can they live a life of true abundance? The first step is to be honest and look in the mirror. What do you need to learn so that you can teach your children? It's okay if you don't know everything. Your children will respect you if you learn with them. Never started a business? That's okay! Not sure what are the best mutual funds to buy? That's okay! Never invested in real estate? That's okay too! The process should be fun, and you can learn and teach your children.

Now I'm going to walk through five specific steps that you can start doing today. You can teach your children about money and set them up for a lifetime of financial success.

BEFORE WE GO THROUGH THESE FIVE STEPS, I SHOULD START WITH THE FOUNDATION— COMMUNICATION!

You must be comfortable talking about money. Explaining how a credit card works, the cost of food, camps, etc. These are important lessons. Note that we don't share specifics. We don't tell our boys how much we earn or what our net worth is. But if they want to know how much our car cost, we will tell them. With the Internet, they can find these things on their own, so why make it a secret? Now onto the next steps:

1. START BANK ACCOUNTS

This is the easiest step to implement immediately. If you haven't yet, go to your local bank and set up a "Custodian Account" for your child. Put in money that they receive for birthdays, Christmas, etc. This account will be where you deposit monthly the "salary" that you pay your children.

Salary? Yes, salary.

2. PAY YOUR CHILDREN

We pay our children a $1 per day "salary" or allowance. To get their salary they must do a few things: clean their room, pick up, turn lights off and close doors. Also, they must be respectful. Leaving lights on in their bedrooms, not doing their laundry or being disrespectful to their mother means they don't get paid that day. Buy your children an accounting ledger. Every week you can put in how much they get paid, including any debits for missed days. When you have two children, it's interesting to watch them become competitive with their earnings and savings.

You may be surprised to learn that once your children are about eight years old, they can begin to work for you as well. Follow best practices if you are going to do this. Our boys help out with various aspects of our businesses, including: sending out books, cleaning our AirBnBs, cleaning our company car, etc. Our target is for each of them to spend 10 hours a week on these jobs. We not only have the boys record their hours, but I've also set them up as employees with my company. If you hire your children, make sure you treat them just like you would any other employee and keep detailed records. This is a great tax-planning strategy, and it allows your children to have earned income so that they can do things like start a Roth IRA.

3. TEACH THEM ABOUT INVESTING

How do you teach your children about passive income? If you ask my boys, they will tell you that "investing is money working for you!"

There are two things you can do to teach your children about investing in a meaningful way:

1. *Match Their Savings*

   My boys know that the Family Rule is to "Save 50%." If they get a $30 allowance, they should save $15. I encourage this behavior by matching whatever they save. So, if I pay them $30 and they save $15, I give them a total of $45, of which $30 goes into their savings account that we set up. This teaches them the value of saving in a world that doesn't really provide enough interest to be meaningful.

2. *Start A Roth IRA*

   When my boys began working for me, we set up Roth IRAs. Choose a brokerage that is kid friendly. Personally, we chose Vanguard since that's where we have our own accounts. Make this automatic and easy for your kids. We linked their checking accounts so that after my company pays them, it is automatically moved each month into their Roth IRA. The money goes into a Vanguard Target Retirement Fund. Every month, the boys get their paper statement. We compare how much money their investments made them versus how much they made in their day-to-day "salary" of $1. Needless to say, it's an impactful lesson!

4. START A BUSINESS

Once your children understand the importance of banking, earning money, and investing, it's time to take it to the next level. We did this by having the boys start their own business. Their first business was a jump rope business. I helped them to source jump ropes from China for about $2/unit. They got the jump ropes, inspected and assembled them, and then sold them at our local CrossFit gym for $10 a piece. This has taught them multiple lessons:

How to identify a need or demand.

Putting an upfront investment into a business (they had to spend about $100 on their first order).

Sales—They've learned to communicate to others.

Accounting and borrowing: They borrowed the initial $100 from me (on my credit card) and then had to properly account for and pay me back out of their initial profits. Then, they had to split their profits between the two of them.

Profit vs. salary—now they know they can sell five jump ropes on a Saturday morning and profit $40. They know they would have to work many more hours at a low starting salary to make this kind of money.

5. TEACH THEM THE TRUE VALUE (AND COST) OF COLLEGE

Read this article, "Actually, College is Not Worth the Cost – A Lawyer and Her Money" (**https://alawyerandhermoney.com/ college-actually-not-worth-the-cost/amp/**)

I'm often asked what I do to save for college. I usually respond with, "I don't know if my boys will go to college." Needless to say, this raises a lot of eyebrows! When my boys talk about going to college, I ask them what they are going to study, where, and how much it is going to cost. I also ask them if they'd rather have their own business or work for someone else.

Now, my younger son wants to be an engineer and design cars (he loves cars, building with LEGOs, and is very intelligent). Would it make sense for him to study engineering and pursue his passion? Probably!

My older son wants to go to college to "play lacrosse." Well, I hope he gets a scholarship for that! That said, he's also interested in being a Navy SEAL. There are plenty of options outside of the traditional route that would make good sense.

The point is that I want my boys to understand one big thing —the return on investment (ROI) of college. If they each had $100,000, would they choose to invest it, start a business, or spend it on college tuition? Why?

I see my job being to teach them how to calculate this and understand their decision. It might make sense for them to invest the money then get student loans.

Whatever your family's choice when it comes to college, make sure you don't just assume college is the only choice. Also, be sure you look at all the options as well as financing.

Being a parent is a constant learning process for sure, especially when it comes to a topic as complex as money. Be sure to make money conversations comfortable in your family. Remember that it's okay if you do not know everything about the above five steps. Be honest and humble. This will help your children to do the same. By following these five steps, you can be sure that you will be well on your way to raising young money pros.

BERTIE LE ROUX

This chapter is dedicated to my wife and my kids who taught me to have patience, compassion and dedication. To trust and love unconditionally and sometimes just to cast a blind eye.

UNREALISTIC EXPECTATIONS

by *Bertie Le Roux*

INTRODUCTION

It can be said, and it is a known fact, that our children are our future and how we invest in their growth and development will ensure not only their future, but ours too. I have no doubt that all parents, and I would like to include their teachers here as well, have only the best in mind for them but unfortunately, we do not all have access to the same resources, offer the same opportunities, or can spent similar time with them to ensure that they grow up to be the best adult they can be. Parenting is a full-time job, but life happens and here we are, seeking answers to be the best parent for little Johnny and Mary, as we can be.

In the next few paragraphs, I will be offering some easy to understand, easy to implement and fun answers to some of your challenges but not without a warning that, if you wish to adopt them, you may need to make some changes in your personal mindset to achieve greater success in your role as parent.

WHO AM I – AND WHY ME?!

My name is Bertie Le Roux, and I am an internationally awarded transformational coach and Speaker, an avid radio presenter, a podcaster and a 40-year business veteran.

As late developer, I was bullied at school, told I was a good for nothing by a middle school teacher, suffered a hip fracture that derailed my dreams as a sportsman, almost lost everything twice and have been fired twice—all because I was living someone else's dream—their unrealistic expectations!

So now I've decided to dedicate my life to helping others to live their deserved life with passion and purpose.

I started my professional career as a high school teacher, mostly in boarding schools, dealing with so called "troubled kids" (mostly a product of "troubled circumstances" I should add). Here I spent many hours in coaching (sports), educating as well as honing my skills as their mentor and confidante. In later years, as chairperson of our districts' s Youth Exchange Program, I learned that the challenges we face in my country, South Africa, are global. The question is then what are we doing right and what are we doing wrong if all we can ask is if there is a better way or a right way? When focusing on "Thinking Preferences," however, the end results are neither right nor wrong or good or bad.

UNREALISTIC EXPECTATIONS

What does unrealistic expectations mean?

If you say that someone is being unrealistic, you mean that they do not recognize the truth about a situation, especially about the difficulties involved in something they want to achieve.

Wherein lies the answer then? Understanding the uniqueness of the child would lead to understanding their "WHY." That is, "Why they do, What they do, the Way they do it!" The moment you, as parent, are confronted with that challenge, you should ask yourself "Why you do, What you do, the Way you do it." In the answer lies the solution – that little Johnny and little Mary may differ in how they see and experience life, what their thinking preferences are and therefore, how they respond to life in general.

Can it be that life through your eyes and that of theirs differs? If so, would they not be responding to what comes natural to them which may, therefore, not be the same as your expectations? Are you realistic when you look at them as "clones" of yourself, that they should love what you do, enjoy what you do, or consider their passions to be the same as yours? What if they do not, what if you are a dominant left-brain person and little Johnny is right-brain dominant? That is one of the greatest challenges we all face in life, the fact that we might have totally different thinking preferences, and yes, you are unique as those preferences are very much part of your DNA. Just think about that, could that not be why communication seems to be one of your biggest challenges – at the workplace, with your family/friendship circles, at home with the kids and/or with your partner?

Let me give you another example. Let's assume little Johnny ("the terror") is dominantly right brain and his sister, Mary (the perfect child) is dominantly left. How would you have experienced them to date?

LEFT BRAIN – controlled, structured, neat (room always tidy and everything in its place), disciplined, orderly, love rules and obey them easily, prefer facts and figures, live in the "real" world, step by step instructions, practical applications, timeliness, etc. If friends—prefer one or two close friends. Sports/extramural activities are more individualized. When studying—responsible, disciplined, neat, detailed summaries, at her/his desk and in silence.

RIGHT BRAIN – emotional, music, inclination for disorder, love change, spontaneous, struggle with discipline, creative, imaginative, non-verbal communication, personal stories, graphics, experimental, easily bored, love friends—very social (groups). When studying—prefer to do it in front of TV or in living room or kitchen—where there are people, enjoy music and noise, handwriting—never legible enough for others.

Can you relate to the following three stories? As parents, we compare our kids with one another or with others and with ourselves and often find the differences very challenging and that is not wrong nor unique.

Take little Johnny's room (the right brain), always untidy actually and, by definition, chaotic but that is where he is comfortable, it is his castle, his place of refuge, his world but it seems that everyone else hates that. So, he gets scolded continuously and needs to tidy up against his wishes …. always a battle. Take little Mary's room (the left brain), everything in its place, orderly, neat and a pleasure to visit! Who is wrong and who is right? Before I make a recommendation, just think of the instances where Johnny dares to visit Mary in her room … he feels totally out of place until he has created a bit of disorder there and then all hell breaks loose. It is Mary's sanctuary, and now he turns it into something else, something where he, at least, can feel a bit at home, if not, then he'll simply not visit. Why should he if he is uncomfortable there? And Mary, she hardly ventures into his chaos as she considers it unhygienic even unsafe … and just maybe, that's exactly what Johnny prefers!

As parents, we wish to teach good habits and therefore, most of us hate Johnny's room and when Mom can, she cleans it up and when Johnny comes from school he is, quite frankly, forced into someone else's world .... not his, and he immediately feels that he does not belong and this non-belonging, this disruption of his world of comfort builds resistance that grows over time. It manifests itself in more ways than one, and he eventually may even rebel against those who keeps on turning his world upside down. "Nobody understands me!"

He experiences it, but probably doesn't know how to term his feelings yet as the constant enforcement of someone else's unrealistic expectations rocks his world. The answer lies in allowing "thinking preferences" to take control so that everyone else can appreciate and honor his world as he should others. It is a learning process for everyone, and that is why we talk about "Whole Brain Thinking." Understanding that others are different by being sensitive to their possible different thinking preferences would allow for "communication and responses" in accordance with their preferences. Talk their language, and their response would be "Wow!"

Mom, while we are talking about little Johnny, try to find ways of helping him cope with discipline, rules, hygiene, etc. in fun ways. Do not clean/organize his room in his absence, and if it troubles you that much, just pull the door close so you don't look at it!! And, if you feel you must, make it a fun and togetherness exercise for you and Johnny. A solution a parent shared with me once was that they have put a basketball ring in Johnny's room with a washing basket below it so he could "dunk his dirty clothes" and in a fun way, at least kept that part of his room less messy.

As parents, we need to be fully aware of the fact that we may, unknowingly to ourselves, be "stealing" our children's youth by not allowing them just to be, to experience being kids and not becoming little professionals in sports, music, or academics, etc. and in so doing, they become little model children doing 100% of what you want and nothing that they prefer. The question I often raise with parents are why so many kids become high school or college/university dropouts, and there is so many teen pregnancies, not to mention suicides ... could it be that our teens are living someone else's dream(s), and the weight has just become too much to bear?!

My last story explains what I mean when I talk about unrealistic expectations. To the frustration of many, I love pens and am always buying new ones and treasure those I receive as gifts. I get many compliments on how my pen(s) feels and writes. But the strange thing is that I know, and so you certainly do too, that the pen consists of two primary pieces – the refill which does the writing and the case that houses the refill. What the pen looks like is therefore immaterial as it is only the refill that counts. Therefore, when someone compliments me about how easy the pen writes, they refer to my pen and never the refill.

The very same argument can be made when we refer to our children, what others see and experience is just the pen and we know that our investment in the "refills" has created these fantastic, free-spirited children we have taken responsibility for developing, ready for the opportunities and challenges of the real world out there.

As parents, we need to be cognizant of the fact that we, too, may be applying our unique preferences with everyone we meet. Appreciate what we see in the mirror! When looking in the mirror, we'll realize we might just be only appreciating the external as well!

IN CONCLUSION

Our primary responsibility as parents is to ensure our children's safety and then to give them space to grow and develop at their own pace. Allow them to be moulded into the best adult, partner, employee, and parent they can possible be. They learn through experience and base their future responses on those carefully stored "tapes" in their subconscious minds. Remember that the brain is incapable of distinguishing between what is right or what is wrong, so every experience, the good, the bad, and the ugly get stored only to be retrieved when triggered by a similar experience and they will act accordingly. Know that we are responsible for their future actions too!

Parenting can certainly be a challenge, and with so many influences, options and challenges out there, our job will not get easier, and it might just be getting tougher so therein lies the answers? My experiences have taught me that it lies in understanding and appreciating the fact that we were all born uniquely different, that we were gifted by God to stand out but that society, communities, political and religious beliefs have moulded us to fit in rather than to stand out. By helping our children to grow up in appreciation of their uniqueness and for us to guide them, to show the path we will have done everything we can. That is our calling, and so is the calling of me as a grandparent!

Why do I do, What I do, The Way I do it! Believe it, trust it, live it!

And above all remember the 3 P's – Passion + Purpose = Prosperity (defined as success). Guide them in internalizing this and you will undoubtedly have fulfilled your Parental Purpose.

ON WHOLE BRAIN THINKING PREFERENCES

I mentioned before that as parent we should give our children the space to grow and develop according to what makes them happy and that can be explained by understanding their thinking preferences. Why they do; What they do; and the Way they do it would correlate 100% with their Whole Brain Thinking Preference Profile. As a certified practitioner, I have experienced first-hand what difference it makes when parents and the child understand their respective brain profiles. Communication is immediate as they then speak the right "language" when approaching one another.

Those of you who may be interested to learning more about Parenting with Whole Brain Preference Thinking as a point of departure are welcome to contact me via any of my social media contacts – Facebook or LinkedIn or via my website **www.bertieleroux.com**. You can use that to email me as well. If you use the reference "No Problem Parenting," I'll give you a 50% discount on my coaching/mentoring rates.

ABOUT THE PRODUCER

JACI FINNEMAN is the founder and parenting coach of Hello World, LLC & *No-Problem Parenting*™. She is committed to helping parents become confident leaders for their children, along with finding happiness in their day-to-day routines and bringing peace back into their homes. For more than 30 years, Jaci has worked as a Family Counselor turned Parent Coach, meeting with kids and parents directly in their homes (in person or virtually) and helping them to deal with and overcome their emotional and behavioral challenges.

In 2013, Jaci started Hello World, a company dedicated to empowering parents to become the confident leaders their kids crave them to be through a model she calls *No-Problem Parenting*™. Making an intentional shift in teaching kids and parents how to give "the problem" less attention and instead, focus on the solution.

As a Parent-Coach, Parenting Strategist, Speaker and Leader, Jaci has more than 40,000 hours of experience working with parents and children affected by trauma and mental health diagnosis. Her down-to-earth, authentic and relatable personality adds light, hope, and clarity to her clients. One of 100 first cousins, she enjoys all things baseball, hockey, and dirt. She and her husband of 25 years, live in Central Minnesota with their teenage son.

ACKNOWLEDGMENTS

Thank You to Dawn Cermak, your belief in my mission and encouragement to pursue my dream of building a resource community for parents is the reason this book became a reality.

Thank You to Lil Barcaski and her team at GWN Publishing LLC. Lil took the time to learn my story and purpose for the book; she saw my vision and made it a reality, exactly as I had envisioned. Redesigning my logo, countless hours of editing, teaching me the process of publishing a book, from the bottom of my heart, Thank You!

Thank You to each of the authors who placed their trust in me, believing their contribution would be honored and respected with the sole purpose of supporting moms and dads in their mission to be the best leader and confidants for their children.

Tricia Parido, Sandra Davis, Elizabeth Jacks Scott, Richard Chandler, Patrice Porter, Nina Cruz, Nellie Harden, Michele Benyo, Melissa Deally, Mattie Murrey Tegel, Joanne Light, Jeannie Baldomero, Jackie Bailey, Heather Greco, Elizabeth Bennet, Edina Adler, Dr. J.J. Kelly, Denise Schwendeman, Curt Jordan, Chris Larsen, and Bertie le Roux, I am grateful for each of you.

To the hundreds of parents who have invited me into their homes and trusted me with their hardships. Your commitment to becoming the confident leader your kids crave you to be is commendable and inspiring.

Thank you to my husband Eric, our son Andrew, our loyal pup Bailey, and my closest family and friends who continue to support and love me for who I am. Your encouragement and belief in me have literally pushed me through many fears and helped me become confident in my endeavors.

And finally, to my mom and dad, your leadership taught me how to persevere with generosity, humor, and faith. I love you forever.

www.ingramcontent.com/pod-product-compliance
Lightning Source LLC
Chambersburg PA
CBHW071152130626
46553CB00004B/1621